THE SOUL'S SECRET

by

Professor

Hilton Hotema

THE BOOK TREE
San Diego, California

First published
1958
Health Research
USA

ISBN 978-1-58509-397-7

Published by
The Book Tree
P O Box 16476
San Diego, CA 92176
www.thebooktree.com
We provide fascinating and educational products to help awaken the public to new ideas and information that would not be available otherwise.
Call 1 (800) 700-8733 for our *FREE BOOK TREE CATALOG*.

THE SOUL'S SECRET

1958

By Prof. Hilton Hotema

Chapters

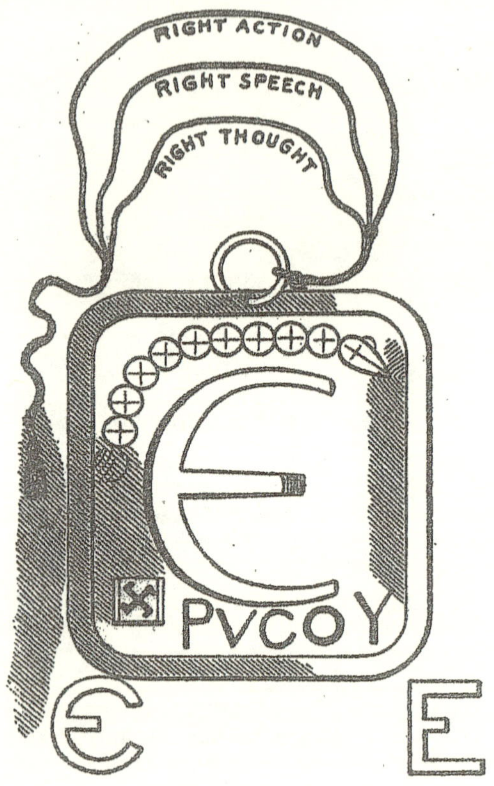

CAMEO TALISMAN OF PYTHAGORAS, PLATO, ST. PAUL, APPOLLONIUS.*
THE LOGOS OR WORD OF THE SIXTH PRINCIPLE
OR TRUE SPIRITUAL SOUL.

The Amulet of the early Christians and Gnostics; the principal gem of the Greek Mysteries; the Delphic E, the sacred number 5, or the five ascending signs of the Cabalistic Zodiac; with the Cable-tow for those who truly enter the Temple, being born again into the *Second Principle of Nature;* the Saviour of worlds and of Men; The Uniting, or the Idea of Heaven; the Unspeakable Things of which it was not lawful to utter; the Seleucidan Anchor; the glories around the sacred person of Man; the Enlightener of Hidden Truth; the Æolian Melodies of Life; the hidden Key to the doorway of the Three Worlds—*i. e.*, Spirit, Elementary, and Elemental; the Lord of all regions; Talisman of the famous Wise Men; Jacob's Ladder; the Self-centred, the Completed Energy; Truth addressing the Godhead; the Divine Silence; the Unspeakable Light of Truth; Cameo Insignia of the Nameless Secret Order in the East

I AM THAT I AM

* On this Cameo Amulet and one small manuscript now held in a monastery in the south of France are based the claims that St. Paul and Appollonius of Tyana were one and the same personage.

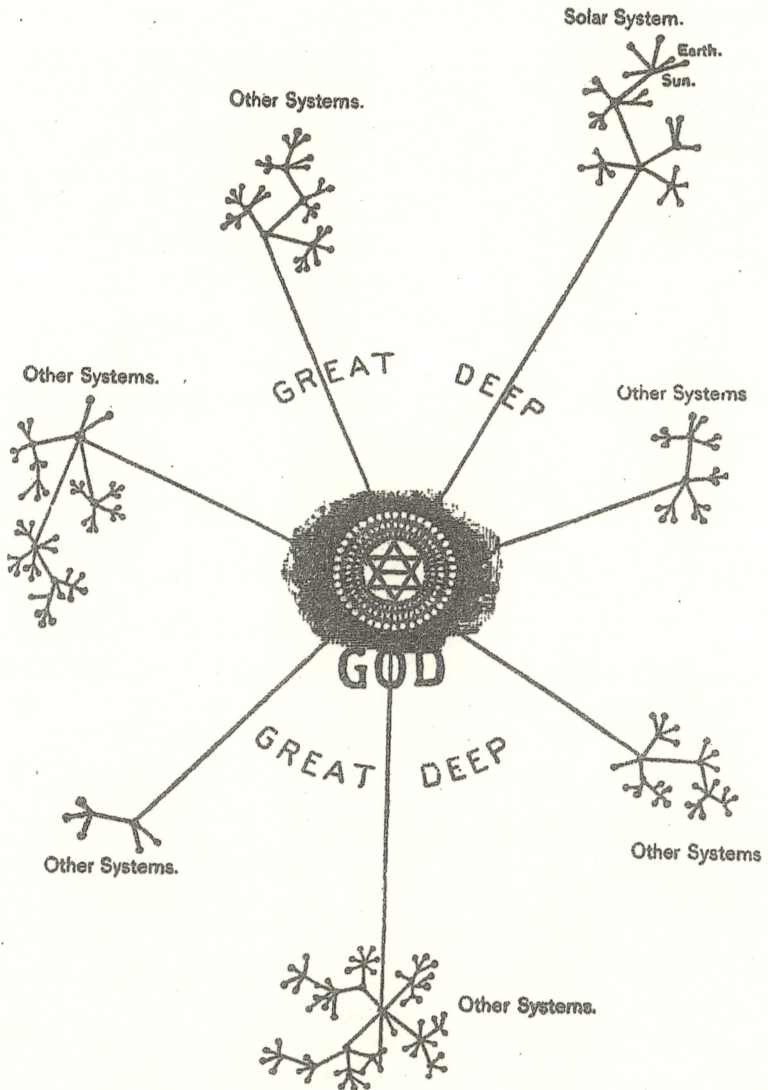

THE GREAT CENTRAL SUN SPIRIT, THE INFINITE AND ETERNAL ENERGY FROM WHICH ALL THINGS PROCEED, THE FOUNTAIN OF ALL LIFE.

FOREWORD

This book reveals the higher science needed to understand the soul and covers its inner teachings. The author states, however, that a complete understanding of this higher science is not possible until one fully grasps the science of the physical world. The first half of this book covers how the physical world works through standard Earth Science. Once this context is established, the author moves into the higher science, covering how it relates to this physical world and offers proof for the human soul.

If one has patience and follows the author's line of reasoning, then a more complete understanding of the "soul's secret" can be reached. The author refers to this higher science as Cosmic Science, which was taught by what he calls the Ancient Astrologers, up until the fourth century AD. At this time, the Roman Church killed many of these teachers and destroyed their work, plunging the world into the Dark Ages, which lasted for a thousand years. Hotema reveals this ancient knowledge in the second half of this book, including how many of these great teachings were incorporated by the Church, but were camouflaged into their texts. As a result, the original teachings lost their power and could only be understood cryptically or symbolically, if at all. The author shows how the books and dogma of modern religions have replaced the deeper wisdom previously attained through actual spiritual experience. He reveals much of this wisdom, which covers proof of the human soul, the survival of bodily death, and the hidden power we have within us.

During the course of this book Hotema will occasionally reference other books he has written. In doing so, he refers to himself in the third person, a scholarly habit he employed that should not cause the reader concern as to his authorship of this title.

Paul Tice

INTRODUCTION

A brief description of the origin of man appears in the Bible, but it was never copied from ancient scrolls. According to that description, God formed man of the dust of the ground, and breathed into his nostrils the breath of life; and man became a living soul (Gen. 2:7).

The Soul has a beginning. It comes into existence as a result of respiration. That makes the Soul a product of body function,--and that is the conception of physical science.

If that be true, then physical science is right in holding that when body function ceases, that is the end of the existence of the Soul.

The biblical makers created an exception to this law. They said that if man will entertain and embrace a certain belief, all will be well and the reward will be "everlasting life" (Jn. 3:16). A very great treasure for so small a price.

This logically means that a belief has the power to transform mortality into immortality. The Soul that would otherwise perish, is raised to Immortality.

If the body were the cause of the Soul's existence, the Soul Would be temporal as the body is. When the body dies, the Soul would perish. For no effective state can stablize itself. An effect depends upon a cause, and when the cause comes to an end, that is the end of the effect.

Much nonsense has been written thru the centuries by many authors to explain the eternality of the Soul. Their work is largely worthless because they cited ho law nor creative process for the purpose of corroborating their claims.

Man has been intuitively led to believe in survival after death. He has had a feeling that made him dimly aware of it, or at least, spspicious.

Down thru the ages these suspicions have been fortified by the experience of sensitives, who "saw things," just as it happens today. Then, man sees in nature that which amounts to death in the fall and revival in the spring of all vegetation.

Man cannot believe that he is inferior to the plants of the earth.

Be not discouraged with life, nor fearful of the future. And entertain no stupid "belief" in order to gain "everlasting life." Neither be a slave of the church in order to escape the torments of its hell.

In this dark hour, when doubt, fear and perplexity are everywhere rampant, it is well to remember that Man, the King of the Universe, who is the perfect embodiment of all living formations below him and above him, and who has dominion over every living thing upon the earth, according to the Bible itself (Gen. 1:28), is not at the mercy of paltry human endeavors, nor in need of a Savior.

In spite of the frightful trachings of the Church, it is well to believe that the Great Power that briggs man into being, does not desert him at birth, and leave him as a helpless creature, according to theology, to be tossed about by the whims of capricious tyrants, who rule him during his life on earth, and make many believe their rule reaches beyond the grave.

Astrology

Ancient Astrology, so bitterly condemned by the Mother Church, dealth with the Celestial Bodies, including the Astro-Egoical Body of Men.

Astrology traced the Astro-Egoical Entity from the Celestial region to the terrestrial world, and explained the process by which the Celestian Ego appeared upon the Terrestrial plane, clad in a garment that harmonized with its physical environment, establishing perfect correspondence between the Egoical Entity and its Physical Home.

That constituted the esoteric philosophy of Astrology that was so utterly destroyed by the Roman Army after the founding of the Roman State Church in the 4th century.

The destruction of that philosophy was necessary for the success to the new philosophy upon which the new church was founded, and which consisted of literalizing the parables and personalizing the symbols.

The Mysterious Soul

By the logical citation of law and analogy, we shall prove in these pages that The Mysterious Soul is not nearly so mysterious as we are taught to believe, and that The Future Life is as certain as the rising of the Sun.

We learn from the Ancient Astrologers that the Human Ego, an Eternal Entity, is the Real Man, without beginning and without end, and moves in the same Cosmic Cycle as the Cosmic Elements which constitute all phenomena, both physical and metaphysical.

The Cycle of Life unfolded in this work is the result of years of investigation and research, and was common knowledge for thousands of years, until the fourth century, when a shocking event occurred which changed the whole history of all countries controlled by the mighty Roman Empire, blotting out the Ancient Wisdom and plunging man into intellectual darkness.

As the darkness slowly receded and an infant science was born, the Mystery of Life was explored, and out of this exploration came the Philosophy of Evolution in the 19th century.

This philosophy reverses cosmic law and order by considering Life to be nothing more than the function of the body, and holding that when body function ceases, Life comes to an end.

It is our purpose to show by cosmic facts and logical argument that Life is not the product of body function, BUT THE CAUSE OF IT. Life does not end when body function ceases, but body function ceases when Life leaves the body. The Evolutionists have the facts reversed.

The facts of Life described in this work were discovered by the Ancient Astrologers, who developed the only Science of Man which the world has ever had, and the only Science of Man which the world has today.

"The greatest testimony to the truth of Astrology is that it has never halted, but has come undeviatingly down thru the ages, down out of the mist of time thru the ancient world and the medieval night of horror, persecution, faggot and blood, from the prehistoric and ancient plains of Chaldea and Assyria to our present time" (British Journal of Astrology).

THE LIFE CYCLE

We shall show in this work that Astroligical Science expounds more intricate cosmic and evolutionary data regarding Life than the greatest of all modern scientists has yet discovered.

The Water symbol of the Astrologers was designed to represent the second of man's constitutional principles, the emotional nature, because Water is so closely inwrought with the physical body as generally to include the latter in its reference.

This is the most suggestive and fruitful use of Water as a symbol. It is the water of earth, of sense, of generation, and it holds the threat of drowning the god. It is the Water on which he must learn to walk without sinking, and symbolized by the gospel Jesus when he walked on the water (Mat. 14:25).

Water is the most applicable symbol of man's lower nature because of its fluidic character and its constant motion and fluctuation, representing sense and emotion.

The Human Ego, cast amidst the senses and the feelings, is in unceasing flux, as Heraclitus said. Like the restless waves of the sea, it is never still. No symbol could better represent the dual sense-emotion-life of man than the heaving bosom of the ocean.

Natural phenomena presents, in the water-circulation system, a marvelous textual illustration of the whole Life Cycle Process.

The ocean is the source of all rising water emanations. The sun raises hugh masses of moisture into the sky by its thermal power; and a reduction of temperature causes the vapor to condense and fall as rain. From remote highlands the water flows into brooks, rivers, and bays, and finally returns to its home in the ocean, ready to make another cycle.

This circuit of water bristles with analogies to the Life Cycle at every turn.

The sun's function of lifting masses of invisible vapor into the sky, symbolizes the Ego's power to refine the unseen elements of Consciousness-Mind-Intelligence and elevate the substance of life.

We must be particular to observe that every phase of the cycle is visible except that one in which the water, as invisible gapor, is lifted up from the sea again into the sky.

The entire circuit of the Life Cycle is perceptible except the one arc in which physical substance is returned to radiation (invisible vapor) form. In every round of cosmic processes, there is always the one stage that is invisible.

This cosmic fact holds a pointed moral for physical science. It has been the stubborn unwillingness of physical scientists and evolutionists to recognize the reality of the Life Cycle in its invisible stage that has kept the modern world in darkness and confusion as to the Soul's Secret, and produced the illogical, unscientific theory of evolution.

This is the point where physical science holds that when the body ceases to function, that is the end of everything. This is the point where we meet the invisible stage of the Life Cycle.

Soul's secret

The fact of the Future Life rests on the law that human life runs a cycle similar to water, issuing from the subjective radioactive realm into the objective, palpable live of the body, and retiring again to the invisible astral plane.

Like the invisible vapor rising from th ocean, the Human Ego rises from and leaves the dead body and returns to its eternal astral home, and its positive existence there is unseen.

So, physical science stands firm on its denial of the Human Ego's subsistence after death on the sheer ground of its invisibility, its disappearance.

Physical science creates the darkness in which it lives and moves by refusing to consider that which the scientist cannot see, feel, smell, examine, weigh and measure.

Ancient Astrology taught that, like the invisible vapor that rises to the sky, so also rises the Human Ego, to return again in due time to the earth, and that it must be subsistent in the interim. For if it did not exist, it could not return.

Knowledge of the fact was what caused the church fathers to destroy all ancient scriptures which touched upon that phase of life and man. For if man knew that Life is eternal, the church could not sell him the unscientific, illogical, absurd dogma that he must believe in the gospel Jesus in order to "have everlasting life" (John 3:16). That is the very foundation of the church and its doctrine.

As the water-cycle is complete in spite of the one invisible segment, so also is the Cosmic Cycle of Life complete, with no arc missing.

The apparently missing link is found in the invisible realm. And even now physical science is discovering that the most vital, most powerful, and most dynamic realities, are those of the unseen world.

The Bible says we look not at the things which are seen, but at the things which are not seen: for the things which are seen are temporal; but the things which are not seen are eternal....And we know that when our earthly house is shed and dissolved, we have a building not made with hands, eternal in the heavens (1 Cor.4:18; 5:1).

Water was the first visible creation, and up out of its depths came the emanating gods to get the breath of life.

There is no more astounding replica of this cosmic process, than that furnished unto this day by the modus of human birth.

When the child is born, it issues into life out of a sac of water, and the first thing done by the attendant nurse is to stimulate the latent breathing function.

The Soul's Secret   Chapter 1

THE FUTURE LIFE

Literature that has lasted the longest is that which has been based upon a desire for or an expectation of the Future Life.

More pages of ancient scriptures which have been preserved to our times, are devoted to the question of Life after Death than to the rise of empires, for the reason that empires die, decay and disappear, but in the case of The Future Life, man lives on and on eternally.

So, the big question down thru the ages has been, If a man die, shall be live again(Job 14:14).

The Christian religion is not based upon the Bible. It rests entirely and exclusively upon this statement:
"For God so loved the world, that he gave his only begotten Son, that whosoever believeth in him should not perish, but have everlasting life" (Jn. 3:16).

The biblical makers attempted to support that statement with one in the Mark, to the effect: "He that believeth and is baptized shall be saved; but he that believeth not shall be damned" (16:16).

A person who can think, notices at once that no law nor creative process is involved or cited to support these bald statements. In other words, Christianity is not founded upon law and order, but wholly upon belief.

All law, order and creative processes are ignored and disregarded by Christianity. They are never metioned; they are of no value. This is necessary, for Christianity fails as soon as law, order and creative processes receive attention.

Constantine Grethenbach wrote: Christianity was not born in a manger, but in a sepulchre. From that sepulchre have radiated the Star of Beth-Lechem as well as the Cross of Constantine; while it has also yielded to us the most unscientific dogma of any great religion, viz., that the physical part of man does not perish at death, but revives to everlasting bliss or everlasting woe (Secular View of the Bible, p.273).

Life and Death

The world's history is composed of the issues of Life and Death. All human activities are ruled by the expectation of death. No man, no community, and no nation escapes the shadow. It affects all our acts. It enters into national policies. It is the drop of gall in the cup of happiness. Childhood and animals fear it. Old age dreads it. Even disease, poverty and crime shrink from release by death.

The Soul's secret

Old Age and Death condition all life to a state of restlessness. They color all human endeavors with a sense of impermanency. They deflect the Mind from purposeful living by bringing to our attention the perpetual prospect of reaching the end.

Anticipation of Death increases the apparent value of time. It creates haste. It induces hurry and struggle for early satisfactionsand pleasure. The Bible says, "Let us eat and drink; for tomorrow we shall die" (Is.22:13; 1 Cor.15:32).

The controlling influence of man's nature, the passion for conquest, is increased and intensified by the expectation of Death. The earth has been, and still is, a slaughter-house. Ambition, lust, greed and vanity have set the mark of Cain upon the whole human race.

With the hope of a present material gain and an early personal satisfaction, but in ignorance of the certain penalties, men have ruthlessly inflicted death and destruction upon one another.

Only actual knowledge of future penalties and fruitions can properly check the suffering and injustice which this passion for conquest entails.

Love of life inspires every living thing. Man alone possesses that high degree of intelligence which inspires the hope of Immortality.

Practically all men desire to live on after somatic death. Most of them hope for such a life. Many have faith. Christianity teaches that only thru belief in its Jesus can the future life be gained. Explode that dogma and Christianity is sunk.

Hope and Faith

Hope is not faith, and faith is not knowledge, yet both are inspirations of life. Hope is but a fleeting intuition, while faith is the steady expectation of the heart.

Hope for and expectation of a Future Life appear to be almost inseparable from human intelligence. In this desire and expectation, the savage, the sage, and the child find a common ground.

Except for this natural hope and expectation of a life beyond the grave, man could not properly formulate his destiny upon the physical plane.

Faith is a perpetual inspiration, while skepticism clouds the best efforts. The creed of the materialist and the evolutionist of annihilation in death saps the springs of human energy, and thwarts the finest possibilities.

The Soul's secret

Do not these facts testify to the importance of the subject? Do they not justify the most vigorous search thru Nature for actual evidence upon this great question of Life and Death?

Who can doubt that such knowledge would rule and exalt the purpose of Life as no fitful hope nor wavering faith can do?

The sacred writings of the ancient nations antedate secular history. The greatest of profane writers have speculated upon the Immortality of man. The works of Plato represent a great intellignece inspired by a hope of Immortality, while the Psalms represent that same hope supported by faith.

It is as natural to desire Life after somatic Death, to hope for it, to seek knowledge of it, as it is to desire food, light and air.

It is an unfortunate man who does not hope for The Future Life. It is an abnormal one who does not desire it. A man without hope or desire merely exists. He can scarcely be said to live.

He who gives heed to his own astral intuitions is never without hope. He who has hope may acquire faith. He who has both hope and gaith my acquire actual knowledge, provided he has the intelligence, the courage and the preserverance to discover the Law of Animation.

Intuition

The expectation of a future life comes first to man as an intuition, produced by the pituitary gland of the brain. That purely astral intuition is as strong in the savage as in the seer.

When physical science is directed to note this fact, it dismisses the fact as "superstition."

This universal expectation of a future life rises out of conditions that are distinctly not physical.

Had the human mind depended upon only physical facts and the rational processes of the Five Senses of the brain for the development of a belief in a future life, it had never developed.

No man who has gazed upon a dead body could ever have conceived the suspicion of a future life.

In spite of the fact that terrestrial life is a veritable house of decay and death, the expectation of, and faith in, a future life have increased with the higher development of man's intelligence.

Hence, it is evident that this faith and expectation are

based in the astral intuitions of all mankind. It is also evident that such faith and expectation are not the mere superstition of savages, for they increase with the higher stages of intelligence and moral life of man.

However, it may have been this astral intuition of primitive man that laid the foundation of the Ancient Wisdon, so clearly expounded by Hotema in his various works.

Man is a rational as well as an intuitional being. He alone is capable of reasoning upon his own intuitions and inspirations. He alone has the intelligaace to seek a rational explanation of these intuitions and inspirations. He alone demands that the Universe shall yield up the secrets of those mysterious hopes, fears and expectations which alternately inspire and terrify the Ego.

The Ancient Mysteries

The astral intuition of the savage established the expectation of the future life. Later, the higher intelligized man attempts to verify his own intuitions by rational means. This destruction by Constantine and his successors was one of the worst calamaties that ever befell humanity.

How well man has succeeded was shown in the progress of ancient philosophy. It was this natural desire for positive knowledge of the Future Life that inspired human intelligence ages ago to begin a systematic investigation of Cosmic Laws.

It was man's resolute determination to solve the mysteries of Life and Death that evolved the great schools of antiquity, which the Roman State Church destroyed in the 4th, 5th, and 6th centuries.

That early effort and ultimate victory are prehistoric events. That is to say, there are now no records of the Ancient Mystery Schools that are accessible to the world at large. But those records have not been destroyed, even though the sea may now cover the continent upon which that history was made.

Man, nations, and even continents pass away, but human effort is never wasted when pursued in the proper direction. Knowledge based upon the ture facts of Cosmic Law is never entirely lost.

Centuries have rolled into cycles, but that Ancient Wisdom has been preserved, transmitted and simplified.

That Ancient School of Life Science has never disbanded. For ages its secrets have passed on only "from mouth to ear." And today Cosmic Science is broadened and enriched by all that past effort, gain and achievement.

Occult Science

Human intelligence, from the beginning, has occupied itself with speculations, hopes, and fears as to a Future Life.

Man of the highest intelligence have employed their abilities to elucidate a reasonable theory looking to life after somatic death. This desire of life beyond the grave evolved and still maintains the pursuit of occult science.

The original secrecy of that school rose from popular ignorance and prejudice against metaphysics. As a result, the facts concerning Astral Life were imparted to the few, and this knowledge was preserved and concealed from the eyes of the world.

It has been only the few who have possessed the requisite capabilities for investigating and demonstrating the fact of life after somatic death.

For ages these few sought only to gain and preserve this knowledge. They sought only an individual experience and an individual power of the finer forces of the Universe. It was a later consideration and a broader experience that induced them to impart their knowledge to other men.

Then it came to pass that they saw it was their duty and privilege to impart their philosophy to the world as fast as the world would receive it.

These are statements which will be vigorously denied by both modern theology and physical science.

These critics will oppose the position of this work from different viewpoints. While both will declare that exact knowledge of the Future Life is impossible, each will advance a different reason for this alleged impossibility. The one regards such an assumption as sacrilege. The other scouts the idea as superstitious folly.

Between the bigotry of faith without science, and the bigotry of science without faith, truth runs a terrible gauntlet in this world.

Belief and Knowledge

The great body of human intelligence proceeds along two lines of investigation. The one system is speculative and astralistic. The other is scientific and materialistic. The one represents intuition unsupported by reason. The other represents reason unaided by intuition. The one stands for only astral perception of ethical principles. The other represents only rational conceptions of material facts.

In its expectation of a Future Life, mankind as a whole is sustained by faith and not by actual scientific knowledge.

The Soul's secret

The creeds of Christendom all begin, "I believe."

Not one begins, " I know," when referring to the Future Life.

By the adoption of such a creed, theology ranks as speculative philosophy. This is true of any religious system that offers no rational means for demonstrating its dogmas.

Physical science is based upon the facts of physical phenomena rationally demonstrated. It rejects that which is not susceptible to demonstration. It would not be science without adopting this course.

Physical science is right when it refuses to accept as science that which is undemonstrable. It errs when it seeks to dogmatize as to what is and what is not demonstrable as to man.

Theology rests upon intuitions, and faith in those intuitions, while physical science is built solely upon physical phenomena and the demonstration of physical facts.

The weakness of theology is its ignorance of physical phenomena. The weakness of scientific skepticism is its contempt for the supernatural of theology. Both systems, being human, are paralyzed by narrowness.

The clergy no longer is able to deny the facts of physical science, and the foremost specialists of physical science are secretly studying the psychic forces in Nature.

Theology is hampered by the fear that science will uncover theological errors. Science is supersensitive as to any criticism of its deductions and theories.

Intuitions of a Future Life are not proofs even to the rational mind. Intuition cannot be classes as knowledge. It is a suggestion of knowledge that may be acquired.

People in general know the potency and inspiration of intuitional perceptions which are not explainable in reason. While intuition is not knowledge, yet it is a higher guide in life than is cold reason when it entirely ignores these convictions of the Ego.

For many centuries controversy has raged as between speculative theology which teaches life after physical death, and speculative philosophy which teaches that death ends all.

With a Luther, Calvin, Knox and Wesley on the one side, and a Voltaire, Spencer, Schopenhauer, Kant and Renan on the other, it is little wonder that lesser lights become confused as to this question of the Future Life.

Physical science augments this confusion. It enters the debate with demonstrated facts which dismay theology and dis-

The Soul's secret

concert metaphysics.

Part of these discovered facts contradict certain theological dogmas. So, physical seience declares that theology has no basis in fact. By this course it assumed there can be no undiscovered facts which might demonstrate the astral side of cosmic processes. Instead, physical science assumes that there are in Nature only physical facts and physical forces, and that theme facts and forces are demonstrable by methods of physical science alone.

If the Christian world really knew what it now only professes to believe, very quickly the whole existing order of theological discourse would change, and its Jesus disappear.

If physical science were only able to conceive that there might be facts lying beyond the scope and methods of its own schools, how soom would our general scientific study and experiments include the psychic phenomena of life.

As it is, both theology and physical science agree in declaring that human intelligence cannot penetrate further into the secrets of the Cosmos.

Who can estimate the benefits that would flow from the exchange of mere faith in a Future Life for actual knowledge that such is a fact? But that would destroy the very foundation of Christianity, for which reason Christianity opposes it. The Anceint Mysteries possessed that knowledge, so, they had to destroyed to make the world safe for Christianity.

The church professes this faith only on the conditions contained in the New Testament. If you believe in its Jesus, you shall not perish, but have everlasting life (Jn.3:16).

If the millions of Christians could really know that life beyond the grave is a fact, the whole dismal paraphernalia of death, along with the gospel Jesus, would disappear.

If men entertained even an unwavering faith, their lament for the dead would be greatly modified.

The truth is, the professing Christian mourner exhibits but little greater foritiude and faith when death claims a friend than does the average unbeliever. The Christians mourn their dead with an abandon that demonstrates the instability of their faith.

If one really believes in a Future Life, there is neither reason nor excuse for this intemperate grief.

If a man could know what he but mournfully hopes, the house of the dead would never be a house of despair. Instead, it would be a house of unselfish rejoicing whenever death released the Ego from old age, sickness or sorrow.

The Soul's secret

When man knows what somatic death really is, he will never retard the passing Ego with selfish grief.

If women possessed the faith they claim, they would not swathe themselves in unsanitary crape nor visit cemeteries to commune with the dead who are not there.

To him who knows, the dead body is but the discarded mantle of his friend, one that had served the terrestrial uses of Ego for the time. As such, the body is entitled to due reverence and is consigned to the earth or the fire without exaggerated grief. But not sooner than three days after death.

Theology Fears Facts

If theology could rationally demonstrate a basis for its faith, life on earth would be transformed with new and higher impulses and aspirations. On the other hand, if physical science could prove its own major premise, viz.,:"All is physical matter and mechanical energy," the church would have a hard struggle to survive.

While science drives theology from one false position to another as to evolutionary history, it does not in the least affect the basis of theology, nor arouse the masses and make them think.

For the sake of its own safety, theology is not disposed to make a rational effort to verify its faith in the Future Life. But physical science has conducted a determined campaigan against what it terms the "superstitions" of mankind.

Physical science has made a vigorous effort to substantiate its declaration upon this question. The special point of attack has been modern spiritualism.

Modern Spiritualism

A long and critical investigation has been made of those peculiar phenomena which attach to special mediumship. The purpose has been to show that such phenomena are the result of trickery, or are brought about by certain peculiar physical and mental powers resident in and natural to the alleged spiritual medium.

That effort has been a lamentable failure. The insufficiency of either the charges made or the methods used by physical science is clearly demonstrated.

Modern Spiritualism, embracing millions of followers, has risen during the past seventy years in the very face of scientific skepticism.

Mesmerism, once decrided, is now introduced as hypnotism and practiced by the "regular" schools of medicine. They will try anything in their struggle to save medical art against the rapid growth of drugless systems.

The almost simultaneous birth, rise and spread of Theosophy, Christian Science and Mental Healing among intelligent people are phenomena which physical science has not tried to explain. Much of it is due to the tragic failure of medical art.

Newspapers, reflecting the average mind and practice, publish almost daily accounts of faith healers, of mind reading tests, of telepathic incidents, and of the varied phenomena attaching to hypnotism, clairvoyant, clairaudient, and impressional meduimship.

Persons possessing psychometric powers have been called upon to aid in the detection of crime, while the defense of the criminals on the ground of "hypnotic control" is growing more frequent in legal procedure.

The courts have been compelled to take judicial notice of the existence of hypnotism as a fact.

These facts constitute a very substantial answer to that fundamental dogma of physical science which declares that "All is physical matter and mechanical energy."

The failure of physical science to prove this proposition is confesses by every specialist who has made a personal investigation of Modern Spiritualism.

Notably among these are Prof. Wm. Crookes, F.R.S., and Alfred Russel Wallace. Both of these scientists began their investigations in a skeptical frame of mind. Every experiment and dogma of physical science known to them was opposed to the idea of metaphysical forces and of physically disembodied intelligence.

Both of these scientists entertained the belief that the complete exposure and utter route of Spiritualism depended simply upon a few scientific tests directed by the rational mind of a physical scientist.

The results are too well known to require discussion here. Both of these prejudiced representatives of physical materialism confessed failure. Both have publicly admitted that the phenomena of Spiritualism are facts in nature which defy the analysis or explahation of physical science. More than this, both agreed that such phenomena are due to metaphysical forces and to physically disembodied intelligence.

These cosmic secrets Prof. Hotema has explained in "The Flame Divine" and the "Pre-Existence of Man."

Having employed every test known to physical science and reason, these master minds of modern science have satisfied themselves that somatic death does not end all.

And how has the body of science received that patient inquiry and cheering message? Just exactly as the learned of the time received the messages of Copernicus, Galileo, Harvey, Franklin, Gray, Argo, and others.

Both Crookes and Wallace have been overtly ridiculed and declared to be insane by these professed scientists who have not taken the time and pains to investigate the facts for themselves.

This is the reward of two intelligent men for reporting honestly upon the results of their scientific investigations.

Chapter 2

What Is Life

No definite, satisfactory postulate of man and the Future Life can obtain as long as the genesis of Life upon the earth is shrounded in darkness.

Who is not puzzled by the meaning of Life, and its possible continuance beyond the door of death?

The real factors and causes of man's existence are contained in the question of Life itself. And modern biologists to whom the world looks for knowledge on this deep subject, vie with one another in confessing ignorance as to the nature of Life. The great cosmic ray scientist Millikan wrote:

"I cannot explain why I am alive rather than dead. Physiologists can tell me much about the mechanical and chemical processes of my body, but why I am alive they cannot say" (Collier's, Oct. 24, 1925).

Physical science is perplexed. The best it can do is to begin with a primordial life cell demanding nutrition and capable of reproduction. From this life cell and these physical functions, plus a "hostile environment," it evolves man physically, intellectually, and morally.

This theory does not explain the origin of the cell itself, nor the nature of the cause which produced it. It does not explain the original division of living things into male and female. It does not explain the phenomena of consciousness and intelligence which appear in the operation of all living things.

On the contrary, instead of explaining these problems,

physically science most unscientifically relegates them to the region of the "Unknowable."

As to the matter of a "hostile environment," we shall show that here again physical science is in error. Living things do not appear in "hostile" regions where the elements oppose their coming.

The vital problem in sċience is the original appearance of Life.

Physical science confesses itself baffled at every point when it would explain how Life evolves from non-life, how sensation evolves from non-sensation, how intelligence rises from non-intelligence, how consciousness rises from non-consciousness.

Biologists have traced physical man thru the lower forms of life. But they have not mastered the secrets of Life, mind, consciousness, intelligence, intuition, reason, or sensation.

The vigilant biologist traces life to the nucleated cell. Here in the department of Protozoa he becomes bewildered and gets lost. He misses the connecting link. He cannot discover that subtle element which enters into and converts inert matter into the nucleated life cell.

The biologist examines a cell which may be either animal or vegetal. He cannot feel, see, weight nor measure that which differentiates the simplest form of animal life cell from a vegetal cell. His science cannot determine as to whether certain cells will germinate vegetal or animal life.

The Darwinian theory of evolution depends upon the original hungry life cell. This theory does not account for the hunger fo that cell any more than it does for the origin of the cell itself. Even the quality termed "hunger" may be a myth of the imagination.

Darwinism declares that everything came to be as it is because it was reinforced from without, and because hunger and a hostile environment forced it to do thus and so.

All of this appears as mere word-play to conceal ignorance.

This assumption accepts both hunger and life as ultimate mysteries, and concerns itself entirely with the physical phenomena manifested by this unexplained hungry cell after it is generated by an unknown force.

Physical science here rests upon the assumption which precludes further investigation as to the genesis of Life. Failing to account for it by the means known to physical science, it holds that it cannot be accounted for in science. It contents itself by assuming that Life in some way generates thru chemical, mechanical and non-intelligent physical forces.

Osler held that Life is merely "the expression of a series of chemical changes", while Prof. Le Conte said that Life is produced by decomposition. He made this statement in his book on Life:

"Whence do animals derive their vital (Life) force? I answer, From the decomposition of their food and the decomposition of their tissues" (p.188).

With this for a major premise, physical science is thereafter forced to assume that all further evolution or organization or variation of Life Cells rests upon chemical, mechanical, and non-intellectual physical movement.

Physical science is thus constrained to assume that man is the direct product of a blind digestive apparatus, thus making doctors believe that failing appetite is a cause for alarm, and that fasting the sick is dangerous. At the same time there is evidence presented by Hotema in "The Facts Of Nutrition" which shows that people have lived for months and years without eating any kind of food.

The materialist simply assumes that the physical functions constitute the sole factors in animal life. He is not concerned with the principle which set the hunger life cell into operation. He fails to demonstrate and illustrate the generation of Life, the pre-existence of hunger, and the original capacity for reproduction.

These assumptions of physical science also ignore that principle of the Universe which endows original protoplasm with the masculine and feminine characteristics, qualities and capacities.

No school of science will satisfy human intelligence which attempts to the theory of evolution without reference to the principles which generate a living entity and endow it with hunger, sex, consciousness, intelligence, and an impulse to persist as an individual.

"The presnet state of knowledge furnishes us with no links between the living and non-living." Thus declared the Encyclopedia Britanica when summing up the value of all experiments thus far made by physical science as to the origin of life.

Generating Life

For years the world of science has harbored the expectancy of generating Life by experiments. Two groups of scientists warmly debated the issue. One group, the experimenters, advanced the theory of spontaneous generation of Life from non-living substance. The other maintained that Life generates only from antecedent Life.

The experiment consisted of sealing boiled water in air-tight jars.

When the generation of Life failed to occur, it had to be conceded that Life does not generate in a vacuum. Their opponents were also right when they declared that Life generates only from antecedent Life.

Upon the strength of these experiments, physical science formulates what it terms the "Law of Biogenesis."

While this theory fails to explain both the principle and the process involved in the generation of Life, yet it does undertake to explain how Life cannot generate.

It claims there can be no passage from mineral to plant life, nor from plant to animal life. It declares that the doors of each kingdom are hermetically sealed upon the mineral side.

"Natural Law in The Spiritual World" by Henry Drummond was a highly popular work in its day that attempted to apply this theory to the spiritual side of existence. The argument is based upon the deductions of Huxley and Tyndall upon this subject.

Drummond took it for granted that the opinions of these great scientists closed the case of Nature; for he said:

"The organic is stakee off from the inorganic by a barrier never yet crossed from the other side." And he added: "No change of substance, no modification of environment, nor any form of energy, nor any evolution can endow a single atom of mineral substance with Life."

That declaration Drummond had never made had he known what Life is, as we shall show in this work.

Physical science is not familiar with the cosmic process by which mineral substance is raised to correspond with the vito-chemical life element. All that physical science has really demonstrated is:

1. Animal life appears in a singel nucleated cell.
2. It contains one substance not found in vegetal forms of life.
3. These cells are endowed with the functions of certain activity and reproduction.
4. These cells have an inherent tendency toward organization.
5. These organisms differentiate and improve in appearance, complexity and capacity.
6. All entities endowed with animal life display intelligence in their operations.
7. Animal organisms successively develop consciousness, intelligence, intuition, volition, reason and morality.

In the final analysis, physical science fails to suggest the cause which produces the original cell. It relegates to the region of the "Unknowable" the origin of terrestrial Life. Thus, modern science, by its own testimony, stands convicted with insufficiency upon the question most vital to all scientific progress in relation to man.

By a consideration of all the evidence, the world should be convinced that no doctor is competent to treat the sick until he knows what he is doing. And no doctor can know what he is doing to the sick body as long as he is in darkness as to the nature of Life.

No doctor would deliberately poison a sick body with his drugs and serums if he understood the cause and nature of illness. Nor would he be so stupid as to suggest the immunization of man against "disease" if he knew the cause and nature of "disease."

And furthermore, it is highly certain that physical science will reject with scorn any explanation of Life and "disease" which emanates from another sourse. For physical science, as a shhool or coterie, is just about as intolerant as were the older groups of investigators.

A certain pride of intelligence has been the great stumbling-block all along the path of science. Egotism and dogmatism appear to be the weaknesses of most great specialists. It seems inevitable that when the scientist finds himself completely baffled, he declares to the world, "We have reached the Unknowable."

When men of science will consent to substitute the world "undiscovered" for the word "unknowable," dogmatism and persecution will have received their death-blow. A pursuit of the facts of the Universe will then replace the mere effort to sustain an individual opinion or the deductions of any certain school or coterie.

Vibration

Thomas A. Edison, noted inventor, declared "All is vibration." He demonstrated that only a given range of vibrations of physical matter can be reported and registered thru the physical senses of man.

Prof. Roentgen demonstrated that there are certain higher vibrations of matter, invisible and intangible to the physical sense, which may yet be dealt with by science. The X-ray is neither seen, heard, touched, tasted nor smelt, but it exists as an acknowledged reality and demonstrated force.

Since the days of Roentgen, other rays have been discovered and added to that class.

In 1957 it was reported that two scientists, working on radar development during World War II, discovered that in less then a minute the invisible radar beam can kill a man. They said that microwaves emmited by a radar transmitter could penetrate the walls of a building and cause instant, intolerable heat in the human body.

The press of Oct. 13, 1957, reported that a fantasic electrical sea surrounds the earth and extends at least 200 miles into space. It has been termed the "Ironosphere," and is said to protect "a fragile world from the searing rays of the sun." Prof. Hotema covers this important subject in "The Flame Divine."

Physical science is making surprising strides in the demonstration of these higher vibrations of substance. It has proven that natural phenomena embraces both Matter and Force which make no impression upon the physical senses of man. By reason of such experiments it has arrived at the point where it could readily extend its lines into the broader field of cosmic science.

Cosmic science demonstrates that there is a world of material vibrations and forces which eludes all physical organs of sensation, all physical instruments of registration, all physical experiments, and all physical means and methods of analysis and demonstration.

That great scientists Alexis Carrel called man's Mind the most colossal power of this world, and added that it is complerely neglected by physiologists and economists, and almost unnoticed by physicians. (p.118).

Physical science agrees that the vibration of substance means the movement of substance. It agrees that this vibration or motion of substance, as a whole, is maintained by the action and reaction of individual particles moving upon one another. Physical science also agrees that by and thru this ceaseless activity of substance, force is indicated and generated.

Thus far physical science coincides with Cosmis Science. But the latter goes much farther along the same lines of experiment.

The Ancient Astrologers went so far as to demonstrate that it is the ceaseless activity of individual particles moving upon one another that refines substance itself and increases its vibratory action.

Physical science is concerned at present with the vibrations of physical matter only. Astrology was concerned with the vibratory activities of astral matter as well as physical material. It studied physical matter by physical means and astral matter by astral means.

Cosmic science goes back to astrological science and is in position to discuss the law of motion and number from two points of view instead of one. It is prepared to estimate and compare the difference in the refinement of matter and the vibratory activities of two worlds of matter.

Polarity

There is so much obtainable knowledge on the astral side of natural phenomena that Cosmic Science is justified in presenting certain astrological principles as universal principles and certain deductions as fundamentals in science.

The Astrological Principle of Polarity is the universal principle under immediate consideration.

Those propositions which relate to the evolution of man rest upon this principle.

Evolution involves the refinement of matter, the increase of vibratory action, the generation of animative force, the individualization of intelligence, and the development of consciousness and mind. These quaternary qualities are what make man what he is.

Those experiments which demonstrate the foregoing propositions lie beyond the present scope and methods of physical science. They are experiments possible only to such as are specially prepared for such work.

These propositions, however, are not intended to explain the principle of polarity itself. They indicate only the fact that science discovers such a principle. They are not intended to explain why the principle governs evolution. They are merely intended to state that, under this principle, matter is refined and increased in vibratory action, that animation is generated, and consciousness, mind and intelligence are attained.

All that science can ever hope to accomplish by mere publication, is to cite facts, state principles, and rationally elucidate them.

The principle to be stated and elucidated in this work is that the principle by which matter is refined and increased in vibratory action thru and by the efforts of individual entities seeking vibratory correspondence in other like individuals of opposite polarity.

Cosmic Science discovers something more in nature than a universal astrological principle of polarity or affinity. It discovers something more than physical matter in motion. It finds that a physical entity is something vastly more than mere physical matter keyed to a certain rate of vibratory action. It finds that all matter is alive, or rather that matter is animated by a force that may be named either electro-magnetism, vitality, or life.

Cosmic Science finds that a steel magnetic exhibits a certain character of vitality. A tree possesses yet another, and the animal still another, while it finds that man exhibits higher and more subtle energies than anything below him.

The Soul's secret

Science demonstrates that in addition to matter, nature embraces certain subtle elements which are universal in time and space, and are defined as Life Elements.

Finite science, be it understood, does not attempt to account for these elements in nature any more than it does matter in motion. It accepts them as universal and ultimates in nature, and works along that hypothesis, It simply classifies these Life Elements along with the other universals, viz., matter, motion, consciousness, mind, and intelligence.

The universal Life Elements are four in number and may be defined as follows: (1) Electro-magnetical, (2) Vito-chemical, (3) Astrological, and (4) Egoical.

Science demonstrates that one or more of these cosmic elements magnetizes, vivifies, vitalizes or animates all physical matter, including the mineral atom, the vegetal, the animal, and the humanal. It finds that what we know as magnetism in metals, vitality in vegetation, and life in animal and man are, in fact, certain cosmic relations established between physical substance and the finer and more subtle Life Elements.

The discovery and demonstration of the operation of these Life Elements constituted part of the occupation of Astrological Science. The range of phenomena included in the operation of these elements extends downward to the unconscious mineral atom and upward to the self-conscious man.

Study of the Life Elements in operation is the study of the principle of polatiry or affinity. Thru the analysis of these elements is demonstrated the fact that the principle of polar attraction inheres in the Life Elements themselves and in the atomic particles.

Knowledge of this fact gives rise to certain other important deductions, viz.,:

1. The union of physical matter and the Life Elements is produced by the operation of that principle of polarity which inheres in the elements.
2. Each Life Element displays dual and yet differing powers of positive and receptive energy.
3. In the union of physical matter with one or more of these Life Elements arise the phenomena of animation (Life).

As stated, most of the experiments which support these statements lie beyond the present means and methods of physical science. But it is possible for the intelligent reader to gain a rational conception of the principles, properties and elements with which astrological science deals.

The four Life Elements give rise successively to the four physical kingdoms, viz., mineral, vegetal, animal and humanal.

Each one of the Life Elements gives rise to a distinctive form of physical activity or life. Each element governs a kingdom that is entirely distinct in physical appearance, characteristics, capacities and conduct.

1. Electro-magnetical, considered the least potent of the vital elements, activates mineral substance and exhibits merely the qualities of union, cohesion and aggregation.

2. Vito-chemical element, the next higher, vivifies vegetal substance and governs a higher state of animative activity. This element displays something more than the qualities of union, cohesion and aggregation. It does something more than to unite already existing particles. It possesses, in addition, the powers of growth and organization. It generates new forms by attracting the essential materials from the cosmic reservoir.

3. The Astrological element, a still higher and more potent element, generates a still higher state of animation. Animal life is a distinct advance beyond vegetal life. Animal organisms posses a vitality,capacity and power superior to the plant.

The animal cell exhibits the same unconscious union, cohesion, and aggregation of the mineral atoms. These cells also possess the power of growth and organization as do plants. But the animal possesses capacities which far transcend those of the mineral and vegetal kingdoms. These qualities are defined as the four basic and fundamental principles of physical life,--attraction, repulsion,volition and sensation.

4. The Egoical Elements, highest and most subtle known to science, inspires the kingdom of man.

In this fourth and highest kingdom appear every capacity, characteristic and power of all the lower kingdoms. Added to these, there is a certain character of life, of energy, and of capacity not exhibited in the lower kingdoms. In this kingdom alone are found, in a patent state, self-consciousness, a rational intelligence, a determinal mind, morality, altruism, and a free and independent will and desire. It is this free and independent will and desire, designed for man's benefit, that have been his undoing.

Thus, each one of the Life Elements dominates a particular kingdom and produces a distinctive class of phenomena.

The two lower Life Elements have a physical as well as an astrological aspect. That is to say, these are the only two of the vital elements that move at such a low rate of vibratory activity as to come within the range of physical experiment.

Considering Franklin, Edison, Morse, Roentgen, Kelwin and Gray as the fathers of electrical science to whom the world is so greatly indebted. Considering the marvelous results achieved by physical science thru its knowledge of the least potent of the vital elements, if is not difficult to conceive of the still more wonderful results which would naturally flow from a knowledge and direction of all the Life Elements.

The Egoical Element is the highest life element with which finite science deals. This is the highest and most subtle element known which enters into the constitution and composition of man.

Water cannot rise above its own source when left to itself. Thus far the Conscious, Intelligent Ego has not risen to an intelligent perception of anything higher than its own self. Some institutions have tried to do it by drawing out of the imagination an entity called God, and endowing him with all the glorious qualities which man would like to possess.

The Ego is the entity most difficult of analysis and demonstration. Study of this entity and knowledge of its principles constitute the highest occupation of human intelligence.

The physical body, tabernacle or temple in which the Ego acts, is the epitome of all worlds and all things. It is the focusing or condensing of the innumerable electro-magnetic currents.

The body cannot reveal thru its senses alone the cause of its appearance (birth), or its disappearance (death), or the reason of its suffering; for it has no memory of itself, memory being stored up in the Ego.

Man contains all the universes, systems, planets, and globes within himself. He is the Microcosm of the Macrocosm, partaking of all life.

The Ego inhabits many globes, and careens thru worlds of experience and draws unto itself a gem-producing idealism from every form of matter. From the lowest to the highest, Man partakes of its rhythm, harmony, or song.

Let us quote an Arabian of the mystic school of Alexandria, Alipilli, an advanced philosopher and mystic. He said:
"I admonish thee that desirest to dive into the inmost parts of nature, if that which thou seekest thou findest not within thee, thou wilt never find it without thee, thou wilt never find it without thee.

"The universal orb of the world contains not so great mysteries and excellencies as a man. And he who desires the primacy among the students of nature, will nowhere find a greater or better field of study than himself. So, with a loud voice I proclaim: O, Man, Know Thy Self! In thee is hidden the treasure of all treasures" (Solar Logos, p.27).

The Hierarchy of the human temple is the Ego. This is the frontier of immortal self-conscious entities, and it lives in its own realm. The personality, the reflection or ray of the Ego, is mortal. But the Ego is part of the sublimer, more astral, more evolved entity which we call the Astral Monad.

He who really studies man, not only considers him anatomically and physiologically, but investigates and analyzes the capacities and powers of the Intelligent Ego, the Real Man, usually called the Soul, and, by some, the Spirit.

Knowledge of the Ego is not gained by merely the dissecttion of the physical body, nor the analyzation of its physical functions.

The several distinct kingdoms of Nature represent the union of physical matter with the several Life Elements. These several kingdoms are seen to rise successively as one after another of the Life Elements are inducted into the physical formations.

Because of so much misunderstanding on this point, we must repeat that the vitalization of physical matter rises from the energies which inhere in the universal elements themselves.

That vitalization does not come from external sources, nor from food and drink as taught by medical art. As Hotema explains in "The Flame Divine," that vitality emanates from the Aeriferous Substance which surrounds the earth, and which contains the Virility of all Life.

That Aeriferous Substance is an animative essence, and of that essence the entire body is formed, being composed of atoms whose terrific power has become partially known to the modern world since the development of the atomic bomb.

As Hotema has explained all this in "The Flame Divine," we shall not go into more details here.

Terrestrial Life is nothing more than the manifestation of certain relations between the animating Life Elements and the coarser physical substance.

The principle of polarity inheres in the Life Elements, which means that what physical science calls the law of vibration is primarily an astrological law, operating thru and upon physical matter.

So, in the Life Elements themselves appears the cause of that universal cleaverage in Nature known as sexuality, polarity, the phenomenon of positive and receptive properties.

Each one of the Life Elements is dual in its nature, and manifests itself as either positive or receptive energy. As a result, the law of polarity, or the law of sexuality, governs everything known to man, from the chemical atom to the intelligent Ego.

The Soul's secret

Unition

Everything in the universe belongs either to the positive or the receptive department of Nature. This applies not only to mineral, vegetal, and animal substance, but also to organized entities, vegetal, animal, and humanal.

Between the positive and receptive energies of any one of the Life Elements there exists an inherent attraction and irresistible impulse for unition.

As a result, all physical substance, entities, and individuals representing those dual energies, are impelled to unition by the affinities resident in the Life Elements themselves.

Thus, each kingdom of Nature is divided into a positive and a receptive department.

Between these two department, between these oppositely polarized, sexualized atoms, entities and individuals, there exists an eternal affinity or impulse for unition.

The science of chemistry is based upon those affinities which inhere in the Electro-magnetical and the Vito-Chemical Life Elements.

The astrological philosophy of life was based upon those affinities which reside in the Astral and Egoical Elements of human life. Theology has done everything in its power to destroy all traces of the evidence of that ancient philosophy.

The process by which physical substance is gradually refined and raised to certain ratios of correspondence with the Life Elements constitute the evolutionary process upon the earth.

The astrological principle of polarity which inheres in those Life Elements, appears as the agent employed by Atomic Intelligence to direct this process.

This principle evolves the four great kingdoms of Nature, successively governed by the Four Life Elements.

Sexuality

According to all sciences, there is a planetary period antedating all forms of vegetal, animal and humanal life on the earth.

During this period, the lowest of all the vital elements directly governed physical substance.

During this period, the cold electro-magnetic forces operate directly thru and upon all physical matter. These forces operate as positive and negative energy, symbolized by the White and Black Serpents of the Caduceus, and the Red and Black colors of a deck of common playing cards. In consequence, all physical substance is either positively or negatively charges with electro-magnetism.

As a result, two important conditions obtain, viz.:

1. All physical matter is electro-magnetic, or mineral matter.
2. A distinct cleavage exists throughout this mineral kingdom, the one part being positively and the other receptively charged with the governing element of electro-magnetism.

The one part, the positive, is in a highly active state. The other, while equally potent, is simply receptive to the influence of the positive side. Between these two parts there exists a universal attraction or affinity. This is the secret of Sexuality. This is the secret of the division of the sexes.

The result of this attraction between individuals in union. When such unition establishes a perfect vibratory correspondence, an equilibrium of forces obtains. The result is a permanent cohesion, or an indissoluable union, chemically considered.

When such unition fails to establish vibratory correspondence, repulsion occurs, and the divorced atoms seek union elsewhere in pursuance of the law of chemical affinity.

The results of these individual efforts of atomic particles for an individual equilibrium is a constant combining and recombining of mineral substances.

By and thru these individual efforts for individual adjustment, new unions of mineral substances are being ceaselessly formed. Gradually these individuals establish permanent unions, after which the same law operates to attract and unite whole groups of individuals.

The combinstions we call chemical compounds. They are the child of the electro-magnetic forces in Nature. Thus was out earth not only, but our entire solar system gradually formed and solidified from incadescent and gaseous substance.

Moved by this universal principle of polarity, that entire gaseous and liquid mass finally settled into solid globes in the order of their individual affinities.

That is the work of the principle of polarity or sexuality.

That universal and voluntary attraction or affinity exists between the male and female, and is maintained, as a whole, thru and by the individual affinities of the male and female animals.

This affinity between intelligent human beings is governed

by that fundamental principle which impels every entity to seek vibratory correspondence with another like entity of opposite polarity.

The result of attraction and affinity between intelligent human beings is union or marriage. Failure to attain the harmonic relation sought, results in natural repulsion, natural divorce, and a natural desire to seek self-adjustment elsewhere.

Propagation

The unition of two intelligent human beings is an expression of cosmic law which seeks to unite the two halves and complete the unit. In that union the power of generation is attained in the supreme effort of the individual halves to perpetuate the race.

However, reproduction in the human race is not the primal purpose of the unition. Reproduction rises as an incidental function, resulting from individual conduct, and may be obviated with great benefit accuring to the individual.

Because of its degenerating effect upon the individual, the function of propagation received the highest study and attention of the Ancient Astrologers. They discovered that it has dual phases. That it may be exercised for propagation, or for the higher purpose of augmenting the individual health and intelligence.

In the latter case, by conservation of the Astral Essence the health and intellectual powers of the individual are improved, with a corresponding improvement in Consciousness that exalts man to a higher plane.

This is the esoteric path to Seership, as Hotema explains in The Great Red Dragon. The story is told symbolically in Tarot Card No. 6. We encounter it all thru the Bible, and especially in the second chapter of Genesis and in the last book of the Bible, which is entirely devoted to it in deep symbol and allegory.

Hotema has covered the subject well in his two works, "Great Red Dragon" and "Son of Perfection," which should be read by every adult.

He who conquers the allurement of generation has graduated in the conquest of his animalistic nature; and supreme chastity was the most glorious crown set before the ancient Hierophants. Candidates for initiation in the Ancient Mysteries were not accepted until they had conquered the generative urge.

Eliphas Levi wrote: "To expend the Astral Essence in human embraces is to strike roots in the grave. Chastity is a flower which is so loosely bound to the earth, that when the sun's caresses draw it upward, it is detached without effort and takes flight like a bird"

Egoical Element

There comes a period under evolutionary processes when animal substance is so refined and the human is so raised in vibratory conditions, that man comes into a natural and harmonic relation with the fourth and highest Life Element.

This is the Egoical Element, universal in time and space as are the lower elements, viz., Electro-magnetical, Vito-chemical, and Astrological.

When this period is reached, the most subtle element in Nature is inducted into the animal man and he becomes the humanal man.

The same principle of polarity which crystallized the fiery cloud mass into our solid earth, continues to operate even after it has perfected all four physical kingdoms and established man as the master of them all.

The arrest of physical instrument of vitality, consciousness, mind and intelligence so far as its mechanism is concerned. Man is now provided with all the necessary organs for the uses of physical, astral, intellectual and moral living.

King of the Earth

Creation furnishes no higher known type in organic form tham Man. He is the King of the earth.

However, man's physical organism is susceptible to immeasurable refinement and corresponding increases in vibratory action, but not to any known change structurally other than the development of those structures.

There is some question here in which scientists do not agree. This is covered by Hotema in the "Great Red Dragon". It deals with the subject of propagation. Some hold that originally, man was a complete, bisexual unit, capable of propagation under the law of parthenogenesis. We shall not discuss that phase of the matter here.

With the arrest of the physical body, there begins a higher evolution of human intelligence. But that state occurred thousands of years ago. Man is not today the equal, intellectually, of the Ancient Astrologers who developed the symbolism which conceals their discoveries as to the higher functions of the human body, many of which are now unknown to science.

Carrellhad much to say on this in his "Man The Unknown." He wrote: "Those (doctors) who investigate the phenomena of life are as if lost in an inextricable jungle...In fact, our ignorance

The Soul's secret

(of the body and its functions) is profound...It is impossible, for the present, to grasp its constitution...Most of the questions put to themselves by those (doctors) who study human beings remain without answer...The science of Man is the most difficult of all sciences...The functions of the most complex organs of the body still remain unknown."

The Egoical Element, though manifesting thru the physical form, yet governs the distinct kingdom of intellectual life and therein carries on the higher evolution of man.

The greatest kingdom in Nature, the realm of rational intelligence and of mental development, is the kingdom of the Ego. Thus, the universal Life Element appears to have special offices in the economy of Nature.

1. To the Electro-Magnetical is assigned the refinement of mineral substance and the solidification of the earth.

2. To the Vito-chemical is given the task of preparing the plant for physical life.

3. The particular office of the Astrological Life Element appears to be the completion of the physical body.

4. To the intelligent Ego is specially assigned the acquisition of knowledge.

From the lowest to the highest, each element has performed its task thru the polaristic principle of positive and receptive energy.

Only by comparison is human intelligence able to comprehend this cosmic drama which is constantly being enacted by the sexual powers in Nature.

Only by comparing a positive and a negative mineral atom with a man and a woman can the mind grasp the tremendous meaning of the work Polarity, and the significance of the term Evolution.

Linneus concisely expressed these evolutionary steps in Nature when he said: "Stones grow, plants grow and live, animals grow, live and feel."

Had he gone a step farther and added: "Man grows, lives, feels and thinks," he would have expressed the philosophy of the Ancient Astrologers.

It requires great effort of intelligence to perceive that all this marvelous movement, change, and progess depend upon that one principle which impels everything that is, to seek correspondence with that which is of opposite polarity. Little wonder that the Ancient Astrologers gave so much time and attention to the study of Sexuality.

Thus, the universal principle of Polarity or Sexuality, recognized by physical science as the law of vibration, is, in reality, the fundamental principle of evolution and the generator

The Soul's secret

of all physical life.

Thus, the philosophy of the Ancient Astrologers is presented to fulfill and not to destroy the laws already apprehended by physical science.

This philosophy is presented that physical science may enlarge its scope, and not to belittle its achievements. We refute only certain theories of physical materialism, and present additional facts to support that refutation.

All that is denied are those deductions which ignore the astrological principles, elements and forces in Nature and assigne the evolution of an intelligent, moral being to the blind mechanical forces of a hostile environment and the function of digestion.

We deny only those deductions which reverse the natural order of cause and effect, and refer that which is astral, intellectual and egoical to that which is physical, mechanical and chemical.

Chapter 3

Evolution

When the Roman State Church was established in the 4th century, the Roman Army proceeded to assassinate the Astrologers and destroy their temples and their scriptures. By the end of the 6th century the work of slaughter, burning and destruction was practically complete.

This marked the end of Classic Antiquity and the beginning of the Dark Ages, which lasted for a thousand years. During that long period of darkness, that mediaeval night of horror, persecution, faggot and blood, man lost all knowledge of himself and of the laws of the universe.

Then came the 19th century, which has been frequently referred to as "The Wonderful Century" because so much was accomplished during this period in the way of discovery and invention as well as of the advance in science and the arts.

The 19th century witnessed such a revolution of human thought that it almost destroyed the God of Christianity, and the Mother Church trembled.

The leading men whose work was responsible for this revolution were Darwin and Wallace, Spencer and Fiske, Huxley and Haeckel, now called the "Fathers of Evolution."

Their theory of Evolution swept the land like a prairie fire. The Mystery of Man was solved. He was an improved ape. Dr. O. A. Wall woote:

"I graduated as a physician from Bellevue Medical College in the same year that Darwin published his work on the Descent of Man; the "Conflict between Science and Religion" which ensued, was fought out and the truth of the theory of evolution was established within the period of my professional career. And with this victory of human thought, many superstitions faded away" (Sex & Sex Worship, p.37).

After the excitement subsided, some of the more sober evolutionists decided to take another look. Two of these were Crookes and Wallace. We have reported above the results of their investigation. Their findings forced them to repudiate the theory of evolution.

Evolution is a word that was given a new definition by physical science.

The dictionary defines the work as meaning to unfold or unroll, as, the evolution of a flower from a bud, or an animal from an egg. It does not mean a change of species, from plant to animal, or from monkey to man.

The principles and processes which constitute evolution had been known to astrological science for ages. Then, why have the followers of the Ancient Astrologers remained silent so long concerning these known facts of creation?

History and experience show that the instruction of people must be conducted within the limitations of the average intelligence.

Scientists have been forced to silence, first, by general ignorance concerning creation, and second, by the general prejudices against those who assume to be the superiors or the teachers of mankind.

The few thinkers who outstrip the masses always have suffered and always will suffer embarrassment in their attempts to transmit their knowledge to the world.

Between the learned few and the unlearned, mind-controlled masses there exist many barriers. There is, first, the fundamental barriers of ideas; next, the barrier of prejudice on the side of the masses.

While the world clamors for truth, the history of human development is a long record of indignities and persecutions which the world has heaped upon its teachers of truth.

No man nor school of man can teach a science or philosophy except the people have reached a development corresponding to the class of knowledge to be taught. Not even then can a people be taught, except by their own free choice and desire.

Picture the perplexity of an Edison or an Einstein attempting to teach his science to native American Indians in their own language. Imagine still further the difficulties, should the ignorant entertain in advance a prejudice against the scientist and condemn his teaching.

The relation between the learned few and the masses has, for ages, furnished a parallel to this hypothetical case.

For more than three hundred years modern science has suferedyjust such embarrassments. It is a continual struggle between the genius who discovers, the ruling despot who enslaves, and the masses which are prejudiced against the discoveries.

Thus has modern science suffered, altho it claims to teach only the visible and tangible facts of Nature, which are demonstrable to any intelligence demanding proof.

The older school of astrological science has a still more difficult task. It undertook to teach the facts of Cosmic Creation which can be personally demonstrated by a higher order of intellignece, courage and preseverance.

The Ancient Mysteries illustrated the gluf between a Master of the higher science and the public mind. A picture of this has been preserved in the fifth chapter of the last book of the Bible, as Hotema shows in "Son of Perfection."

The Book with Seven Seals symbolizes the human body. But no man in heaven nor on earth, neither under the earth, was able to open the book, neither to look thereon.

Wait; lo, in the midst of the throne of the Four Beasts (representing the Four Elements of Creation which we shall discuss in due time), there stood a Lamb as if it has been sacrificed, having seven horns and seven eyes.

The Lamb represents the trembling Neophyte, who has been prepared for initiation in the Ancient Mysteries by undergoing the rigid tests required to prove his worthiness. The seven horns symbolize the seven powers of action, and the seven eyes symbolize the seven powers of perception, as explained by Hotema.

The student should disregard everything said in Revelation about the gospel Jesus, as those statements are spurious interpolations. That book was compiled from an ancient Hindu scroll, written thousands of years before the world ever heard of that Jesus. Hotema tells the story in his "Mystery Man of The Bible," and also explains the astrological meaning of the "Second Coming of Christ."

The Masters of the Ancient Mysteries could no more have

explained the astrological processes of creation to the simple masses than Roentgen could have explained the x-ray to native Patagonians.

The mass intelligence has always been closed to science. People do not search for facts, but for evidence to support their belief. The study and utilization of creative forces have no place in the popular mind. Even the better educated have not studied cosmic processes after the rational methods of the few.

So great has been the chasm between the common mind and the trained intelligence of the few, that no attempt is made in public to teach the science underlying this philosophy.

The deeper teachings of the Ancient Astrologers have been concealed in symbol and parable, in allegory, proverb and song. Only advanced intelligence desires and demands literal and exact knowdedge.

Materialism

Physical science, as its name implies, is concerned only with the physical aspect of the visibel world. It deals with phenomena visible or tangible to the five physical senses. It deals with man, the earth, the planets and the universe wholly upon the physical side. It attempts to confine itself entirely to that which is visible or tangible to the five physical sensory organs.

Physical science has not been able to ignore certain universal phenomena which, it is forced to admit, are "supernatural" or "meta-physical."

In the first place, it has been forced to consider the phenomenon of intelligence which is exhibited by all sentient life.

Next, it has been forced to concede the existence of certain moral elements which distinguish human beings.

Physical science, by its attempt to explain astral and psychical phenomena by physical analysis, betrays its insufficiency in these particular lines.

At the start, these higher phenomena appear so radically unlike physical phenomena, that physical science is driven into a change of terminology. It is forced to select for this higher phenomena a name that shall distinguish it from physical phenomena.

This definition alone furnishes a commentary upon physical materialism which declares as a basic proposition that "All is matter and mechanical forces."

Physical science classifies these higher phenomena of life as "psychical," a term derived from the Greek "psyche," meaning

The Soul's secret

"Soul."

It is not claimed that physical science acknowledges the existence of the "Soul" by its use of the term "psychical." It does by such definition confess that Nature embraces phenomena which cannot be classified as physical.

After first assuming that everything has a physical basis, physical science proceeds to find the physical causes for its "psychical" facts. So long as it seeks only to relate physical cause with physical effect, it is admirable. When it attempts to relate psychical phenomena with physical causes, it is stupidity.

The inevitable logic of such an assumption is to relate intelligence to the digestive organs, and to define sexuality as the efflorescence of physical lust. Against such assumptions, common intuition, common experience and common sense rebel.

The best intelligence of today accepts the physical facts of Nature as collated and classified by physical science.

This same intelligence declines to accept the theories advanced by physical science as to the causes of psychical phenomena.

These hypothetical dogmas, based upon only half the facts of Nature, bewildered even so great an intelligence as Huxley. Having accepted the physical facts of Darwinism, he somehow felt,bound to accept Darwin's speculation as to the causes of these facts.

As a result, Huxley repudiated Nature and denounced it as a monster without a single principle that conserved justice or love or altruism. He forced his reason to accept that which his intuition always denied,viz., that all we have been, are, or may become, are merely the automatic results of physical feeding, breeding, and battle.

No wonder this great scientist declared life an unsolvable riddle, intelligence a delusion, love essentially lust, and morality without the sanction of Nature. It is little wonder that he said, "I wash my hands of Nature."

Huxley did not understand Nature. He did not understand cosmic processes. He though that body function was Life, as physical science does to this day. He did not realize that body function is the work of an invisible cosmic prinsiple.

Upon such extraordinary hypotheses as these, physical science attempts to account for, and to explain Life and Man. These are the theories which stultify intelligence, outrage, conscience, and violate iniversal experience.

Duality

Astrological Science dealth with man as with any other product in Nature. It studied him upon each plane, and explained him in his relation to both the astral and the physical.

Physical science accepts man as the highest product of the physical plane. But it stops there and goes no farther.

Astrological science discovered by logic and reason that man is the highest manifestation upon the astral plane. The greater comes not from the lesser. Man is King of the physical world because he is King of the astral world.

The Bible calls man a living soul (Gen.2:7). He has a dual nature. The one is physical and temporal, the other astral and eternal.

When the student is able intelligently to leave the physical body for investigation of the astral plane, he discovers certain facts that have a bearing as to physical development. Among these facts are:

1. Man is composed of and operates dual bodies, different in refinement and vibratory action.
2. Man demonstrates that the physical and astral bodies may temporarily separate without causing physical death.
3. During such separation, the intelligent Ego is still attrached to the physical body by a radiatory beam called the Silver Cord in the Bible (Eccl.12:6), as explained by Hotema in "The Flame Divine."
4. It is the intelligent Ego that plans for and effects this release.
5. By personal contact and acquaintance with ex-human beings, the student finds that man lives on indefinitely as the intelligent Ego, while his discarded physical body disintegrates and returns to the gases of the Astral Plane.
6. He thus proves that man is an astral being, destined to live indefinitely in the more enduring astral form. He thus proves that man's physical body is built upon the permanent astral form, or that earthly man is the Ego clad in a garment that harmonizes with his environment.
7. What is discovered as to man is true of all living animals. Each is modeled upon a superior and more enduring Ego.

These facts prove that every physical entity is also an astral entity. They show that what we designate as electromagnetical vitality and life, reside primarily in the astral model of living things. Proof of this last statement appears in the fact that the organic life element passes out of the physical form has disintegrated.

Thus, everything in Nature, from the tiny atom to the highest human, is fashioned upon an astral duplicate, as Hotema explains in "Pre-Existence of Man."

These are the facts in Nature which justified the Ancient Astrologers in declaring that there is no death as that term is commonly understood. Death simply indicates the separation of the astral and physical bodies.

The advantage of Astrological Science in the study of Nature was the ability to use the mind as well as the sensory organs. The physicist sees only the physical side of creation. The Astrologers saw with equal clearness the astral as well as the physical.

That astrological method is recorded in the Bible in these words:
For the invisible things of creation are clearly seen (in the Mind), being understood by the things made (visible) (Romans 1:20).

Every physical thing in the physical world is but a manifestation of the potent and more enduring astral elements and forces. All we see or touch or know as physical matter, is simply coarse, physical material which integrates in organic form upon the astral pattern.

No attempt is made to explain the origin of the patterns that exist in both the astral and physical worlds. In a general sense, it is held that living organisms are adaptations; that is, all living entities have, to a certain degree, been shaped to the uses of their environment and the intelligence expressed.

This does not explain why one intelligent entity shapes its body or is formed to exist as a tree, while another is shaped to swim in the water or burrow in the ground.

One who studies the astral side of creation discovers, first, that all operations of living things are intelligent, from plant to man. All activities of animals are governed by conscious intelligent resident in the Ego.

Man, physically embodied, represents all the principles, properties and elements in Nature. He represents all the energies, capacities and activities of the kingdoms below his own. To these he adds the higher psychical power, or the energies and capacities of the Egoical Element.

Chapter 4

Evolutionists Disagree

For years Darwinism filled the world with consternation. But he discovered and presented only a limited range of date. The facts he found were furnished by astrological phenomena, and he was not in a position to demonstrate all the facts he found.

Alfred Russel Wallace, co-worker with Darwin for thirty years, wholly dissented from Darwin's theories.

For fifty years Wallace investigated modern spiritualism, and declared that certain evidence clearly pointed to the existence of an invisibel universe, to which the physical world is altogether subordinate. His work,"Miracles of Modern Spiritualism," stands for judgment rendered after a lifetime of investigation.

So, it appears that the two men who were co-workers in the same field of science and discovered the same physical facts, reached diametrically opposite conclusions as to the meaning of those facts.

The world at large has accepted the doctrine of evolution upon its faith in the integrity of Darwin and faith in his report upon Nature. It accepted the doctrine because it was so destitute of knowledge appertaining to Life and Man.

The average evolutionist is not more prepared to prove the facts set forth by Darwin than the theologian is to demonstrate the dogmas of Christianity as to life after somatic death.

Darwin's Law of Natural Selection is a theory of unnatural selection. It makes organized intelligence the mere puppet of blind, physical forces and of hostile physical conditions.

Natural selection under Darwin's theory might well be likened to the natural selection that a condemned criminal would make if given the choice of death by the rope or the guillotine.

Instead of natural selection, Darwin's theory imposes a series of evils from which the victim, animal or man, must make a choice or die. His law of natural selection involves simply:

1. Blind mechanical forces
2. Hungar
3. Organs of digestion
4. Hostile environment
5. Repeated processes of feeding and breeding.

In the light of such assumptions, man is the automatic product of mechanical principles, blind physical demands, hostile conditions, and competitive processes.

Man comes to be what he is solely thru physical re-enforcement from without, and by compulsory selections brought about by the hostile conditions in Nature.

Man is simply the effect of his digestive organs. He is a mass of inherited impulses, passions and sensations, acted upon by external physical forces, and held together thru processes of digestion.

This is the theory that underlies modern medical practice, and precludes the idea that an organic entity is an individual operated by an individual Will and an intelligent Desire.

Little wonder that medical doctors kill so many of their victims. Recovery under orthodox medical care is in spite of the care and not because of it.

Darwiniwm would be fairly stated if we were to say: "The struggle for self-preservation compels a battle of the physically strong against the physically weak, with survival of the physically fittest as a consequence, entailing the supremacy of the physically strong and exterminating the physically weak and incompetent."

There is one flaw in this otherwise perfect theory, viz., Creative Brocesses refute it.

Science shows that the earth passed from a stage of non-life to Life.

How? By hostility to Life, or by hospitality to Life?

Science admits and shows that the simpler forms appeared first. It reveals a steady ascent from lower to higher forms, from simple to complex. It does not show the extermination nor even the diminution of the lower forms, or of the physically weak.

On the contrary, science discovers an increase of life in the simpler and weaker forms. The earth, the water and the air teem with life in its very lowest form. The earth is alive with animaculae.

If competition instead of co-operation were the fundamental principle in creation, the earth had not been crystallized, the vegetal kingdom had not appeared, animal life had not been possible, and human civilization could not have been accomplished.

If life, from the beginning, were a battle of the physically strong against the physically weak, the weaker insects and animals could not survive nor multiply.

If evolution meant the survival of the physically strongest, mastodons would occupy the place of mosquitoes. When we consider the extinction of the mastodon and the growth and persistence of the mosquito, it shows there is much that is absurd and stupid in the theory of the struggle of the strong against the weak.

Environment

Physical science demonstrates that the earth was once a shapeless mass of fiery gases whirling in space.

It is the triumph of the spectroscope, under the light of scientific intelligence, to have demonstrated to an absolute certainty that at this hour there are in existence other hugh masses of gaseous substance from which other planets are now being evolved.

When the surface of these new planets shall have cooled sufficiently, they will be covered with life as the earth has been. Whence comes that life? Hotema tells the story in his "Pre-Existence of Man."

Darwin's hostile environment as a condition necessary in the evolution of Life and Man is another conjecture that grows more preposterous under rational examination.

The regions of the earth that have produced the great men and nations of history, are the tropical and subtropical and not the ice-bound polar areas. The great philosophers came from China, India, Persia, Babylonia, Arabia, Egypt, Greece and Rome, not from Canada, Alaska, Siberia, Findland, Lapland, Iceland, and Greeland, as should be the case under Darwin's theory.

Life does not force its way into the world against opposition. Life appears where favorable conditions prevail. Hostile conditions do not produce fields of wheat and corn. Life and man are ruled by the same law.

No living creature can come into being until the conditions are such as to bring that particular entity into existence.

For instance, an egg contains the potentialities of a chick. But the chick will never become a reality unless the egg is surrounded by certain degree of heat for a certain length of time. These conditions are so essential, that in their absence the egg will produce no chick. Slight variations in the temperature during that time, either up or down, are fatal to the developing chick in the egg.

After the chick is created and becomes a reality, it will still perish if not surrounded by certain favorable conditions. If the variation from these conditions is so slight as not to cause death immediately, or within a few hours or a few days, then death comes on by imperceptible degrees, by a process of degeneration, creeping over the creature so gradually and slowly, that the facts are not known until the end is near. Then the facts are misunderstood and misinterpreted by an ignorant, superstitious world, and death is attributed to various and imaginary causes--generally termed "disease" by a profession whose members prove their ignorance by the fact that the majority of them die when they should be in their prime.

Man's Native Home

The presence of Man on the earth is primarily and directly the result of hospitable climatic conditions, which drew him out of potential existence in the astral world to actual existence in the physical world, as Hotema explains in "Pre-Existence of Man."

These conditions had to be ideal and perfect, as for the egg and the chick. They had to be favorable to man's earthly existence. Otherwise, he could not have come forth. They had to be free from freezing weather, and capable of producing in a spontaneous manner, all things needed and necessary for his welfare and comfort, or he would have perished. For he was a child in the lap of Mother Nature, unable to produce anything, and wholly dependent upon the power, climate, and environment that brought him forth.

If all the earth were a polar region, perpetually covered with ice and snow, the Germ of Life would still exist, but it could not, under such conditions, evolve man from potentiality to actuality.

Under such hostile conditions living creatures never came forth. In such region they were never produced. The fact that some now live in such a place, is merely evidence of their hardiness. It adds nothing to their life, but take much from it.

No biologist nor geologist searches for the Garden of Eden as being a land of ice and snow. No doctor worthy of the title will tell his patients to go to the Arctic Zone for health. No scientist will say that frigid weather is favorable for living creatures.

The results of every scientific investigation point to a hospitable environment as the original home of man. Prof. Alexnader Winchell wrote: "Man, as an animal, is unclothed and possessed of a delicate skin. All naked land-animals are natives of warm countries; and, indeed, they must be to endure ordinary climatic vicissitudes.

"Man, similarly, made his advent on earth in a region where the elements did not oppose his coming. Primitively, he is a tropical animal, and wandered into the colder zones only as he learned to protect himself by artificial coverings" (Preadamites, p.356).

Of the region where infant man appeared on earth, Prof. I. N. Vail wrote:

1. "The warm green-house climate of the Edenic world is boldly set forth by the writer of Genesis.

2. "There was a warm climate, for man dwelt naked upon the

earth (Gen. 2:25).

3. "There was a paradise--a garden in which grew all manner of (fruit) trees.

4. "It is plain that no feature of the Adamite period is more strongly painted and emphasized than the warm climate of the Edenic world.

5. "Another feature, set forth in language too plain to be misconstrued, is the great longevity of man in antediluvian times. People lived almost a thousand years. Man's physical environment simply impelled long life.

6. "Man's dwelling naked in his Edenic climate says in plain language that there was no alternative of summer and winter. His great longevity is unimpeachable evidence in favor of the assumption.

7. "This eternal summer climate, it must be seen, is necessary to make complete the harmony of the historian's account" (Earth's Annular System, 1912).

Thus does a shrewd student of Nature examine the conditions of that environment where man first appeared on the earth. His conclusions support those of Winchell.

Biologists know that the appearance of Life and Man on the earth indicate the existence of climatic and other conditions essential and necessary for the preservation, propagation and prepetuation of mankind.

In the prosecution of their investigations, these men have taken various routes, but in the end they all arrive at the same point. Their conclusions are:

(a). We are forced to admit that man is indigenous to the warmer regions of the earth, where fruits, his natural food, are most abundant and in greatest perfection (John Smith, Proper Food of Man, 1854, p.43).

(b). In a climate of eternal spring, where snow and ice were unknown, primeval man lived for thousands of years, and the tropical (fruit) forest furnished all the necessities of Life (Otto Carque, Rational Diet, p.173).

(c). The evergreen tropical palm forest is the true home of man, for the great leaves of the palm, always green, are the best manufacturer of oxygen. They are the best purifiers of the air and the natural nourishers of man (August Englehardt, Carefree Future, p.24).

(d). Man made his event upon the planet in a warm climate, and was without tools and without fire. He subsisted on foods spontaneously produced by Nature. These foods grow wild in abundance in such climate, and are still spontaneously produced in such regions. The forests of the tropic abound in sweet fruits and nuts (Dr. Emmet Densmore, Natural Food of Man, 1892, p.223).

The most convincing evidence that has been presented on this point in recent times, appears in the findings in 1938 of Dr. Eugene F. DuBois, Professor of Medicine, Cornell University Medical College, and Dr. James D. Hardy, research fellow of the Russel Sage Institute of Pathology. These doctors, working as a team, discovered that:

1. The "comfort zone" of the human body is between 83 and 90 degrees, when the body is devoid of all clothing.

2. In the "comfort Zone" the Mind is at rest, for it is then not troubled by the necessity of any function in connection with temperature relation.

3. The body is endowed with the power of perspiration to remove escess heat, and thus protect itself in the "warm zone."

4. The body possesses no mechanism whatever to protect it from cold and prevent the drain of its vital heat in the "cold Zone." Its only fense is the involuntary act of shivering as a natural means of quickening the circulation of the heat conducting agencies.

5. The constant drain of the body's vital heat in the "cold zone" gradually weakens its integrity, saps its vitality, and shortens its days.

6. The body is constituted for the "warm zone", for it is better equipped to protect itself in the "warm zone" than in the "cold zone," and in the former zone the hospitable conditions do not drain away the body's vital heat.

From the experiments made by these doctors, they set forth the following conclusions:

1. The "warm zone" is above 90 degrees. Here sweating begins and becomes uncomfortably profuse as the temperature rises. The flow of blood to the skin, bringing heat and moisture to be eliminated as perspiration, may be five or six times the normal.

2. The "comfort zone" is between 83 and 90 degrees. Here, without either sweating or shivering, the blood easily eliminates heat as fast as it is generated in the body, and the Mind, untroubled by the necessity of doing anything about temperature relation, is at rest.

3. The "cold zone" is from 83 degrees down. At 83 degrees the blood flow to the skin has throttled down to a minimum and can reduce itself no farther. There is no other mechanism of the body to reduce the heat leakage. It is here that the body begins to act like a perfect theoretical "black body" or warm water heater involuntarily radiating away heat energy that it can ill accord to spare.

All the body can do then to keep up its temperature is to generate more heat compensating for the constant drain. This it does by shivering, which is involuntary exercise.

If the reader, living in Darwin's hostile environment of ice and snow, has the least regard of his health, he should ponder well the findings of science as to the region where man is made to live.

Do not be misled and believe that the penalty of your transgression of the Fundamental Law of Human Life can be set aside and be relieved by health foods, by deep breathing, by certain exercises, by drugs, vaccines and serums.

The Soul's secret

Doctors and governments have spent billions of dollers and hundreds of years trying to discover ways and means to assist transgressors to avoid the penalty of their errors and acts, but have not been able to accomplish anything in that direction.

Every animal in Nature has its normal environment, and there it lives and thrives unless molested by man. It never of its own free will leaves that environment for another.

Every animal below man is unerringly and completely guided by Nature. It knows instinctively where to live and how to live. And all animals are perfectly fitted to their natural environment. There they remain and are satisifed.

But man knows not where to live nor how to live. He wanders here and there over the earth, living largely in a haphazard manner. He tries to fit himself to various environmnet, some of which are decidedly hostile and detrimental to his health and happiness.

We have here a sad error that seriously needs correction. We must first teach man where he should live before we try to teach him how he should live. We should not attempt to make him fit an environment which he is not made to fit.

Sexuality

Darwin was as badly mistaken in the matter of Sexuality as he was in the matter of environment. His law of natural selection covers also what he terms sex selections.

Darwinism considers sex primarily as a purely physical desire for propatation. Sexual attraction is interpreted as nothing more than a condition compelled by and dependent upon biological need for reproduction.

While the value of sex selection is admitted, the sex relation itself is construed by Darwin to meet the theory of evolution by necessity. Indeed, sex passion and sex love are defined as a "generative mania," by force of which organic intelligence is driven into obeying "Nature's first command-propagation."

Thus, even that profound, polaristic bond between the great positive and receptive powers in Nature, is construed as a relation compelled and forced upon animals and man by a gross physical passion, which amounts to a "mania."

According to Darwinism, sex has no other uses then the physical. Those uses are solely in the interest of the species and not for the benefit of the individual.

When Darwin has thus analyzed sex, he is done with it. Anything higher by way of intellectual or moral improvement, is undreamed of.

So firmly has this unfortunate doctrine of Darwinism fastened itself upon modern science, that one eminent specialist, Letorneau, publicly deplored the monogamous system of marriage. Indeed, he seriously avocated a practically free selection, with the children reared by the state.

So continually has this erroneous sex doctrine been exploited by physical science, that a new moral philosophy is based upon the theory that sex is only a "physical device for reproduction," and sex attraction is "essentially lust."

This unscientific, preposterous view of the sex relation and function is the inevitable result of a science which deals only with the physical side of Nature. This is the logical doctrine of a school which subordinates the astral, mental, and moral development of the individual to the physical improvement and preservation of the species.

Physical science has never yet attempted to define the sex principle Indeed, sex has never yet been analyzed, as a principle, to modern intelligence. It has been taught by science in its physical aspect alone. This is an error of science which is reflected back upon society thru false literary and social doctrine involving sex questions and relations.

The Secret Doctrine of the Ancient Astrologers was based largely upon this phase of life. The Neophyte was taught in the Ancient Mysteries how the Great Red Dragon (carnal lust) devours man by inches, saps his vitality, shortens his life-span, and pushes him into obscurity.

Eliphas Levi said: "To resist the allurement of generation is to graduate in the conquest of the body, and supreme chastity was the most glorious crown set before the hierophants. To expend the life essence in human embraces is to strike roots in the grave. Chastity is a flower which is so loosely bound to earth that, when the sun's caresses draw it upward, it is detached without effort and takes flight like a bird" (Hist. of Magic, 1859, p.134)

Chapter 5

ARCANE SCIENCE

Delving back for thousands of years, in the darkness of past ages, to the lost Continent of Mu (Lemuria), we discover accounts of Rites and Ceremonies of an Arcane Science, handed down from times immemorial, termed the Sacred Mysteries.

When the search is carried into India, China, Babylonia,

Egypt, Greece, Mexico, Guatemala, Yucatan, Ecuador, Peru, etc., we find traces of the same Arcane Science.

The evidence indicates that from a common center the Arcane Science spread over the face of the earth, gradually growing differentiated in detail as ages passed, conditions varied, and the customs changed to meet the changing conditions, and yet, remaining basically the same.

In spite of the work of destruction carried on by despots and those who have tried to obliterate all traces of the Arcane Science, fragments of it remain, inscribed upon temples, pillars and tablets of stone, and in other places, and may be found all over the world.

This Arcane Science assumed the form of a religious philosophy, and was divided into two systems, esoteric and exoteric.

Many of the secrets of Creation can with profit and safety be given to the masses, but the deeper secrets of Life and Nature cannot be, because they can be understood and appreciated only by those intelligent ones who have made a profound study of the subject, and are mentally prepared to recieve and accept them.

The true essence of the Arcane Science was therefore concealed in symbols and parables, invented by the Ancient Astrologers, and Schools were founded for the preparation of men for initiation in the Sacred Arcane Science.

Initiation was not an instantaneous miracle, but rather a consecutive and gradual course of study, to prepare the mind for a higher cycle of thought and knowledge.

So, the esoteric or secret doctrine of the Arcane Science, when mentioned publically, was veiled in symbols and parables that could be understood only by those whose Minds were illuminated by the Light of Wisdom.

The Arcane Science contained the secrets of Astrology, the knowledge of the Zodiakos, and the epic of the Seven Days and Seven Nights of Creation (Gen.1:31; 2:1-3), which symbolized the Seven Cosmic Forces that govern the action of the Four Great Elements, consisting of Fire, Air, Water and Earth.

These Seven Forces were symbolized as the Seven-Rayed God, concerning which the Emperor Julian (356 A.D.) said:
"If I should touch upon the arcane and mystic narration,... I should speak of things unknown, and indeed vehemently so, to the sordid vulgar (masses), though well known to theurigic and blessed men; and therefore I shall be silent respecting such particulars" (Oration to the Sovereign Sun, p.129).

The Ancient Astrologers taught that the Seven Forces emanate from the Cosmic Unit, as the Seven Colors emanate from clear light. The Seven Colors disappear as they unite in clear light; so, union of the Seven Forces produces equilibrium, inaction, inertia.

It is difficult for the unprepared mind to comprehend that all visible phenomena, called Nature, emanate from the Invisible Aeriferous substance surrounding the earth, and called the Astral Plane. That is the first lesson taught the Neophyte in the schools of the Arcane Science.

The Kabbalah

Antedating the oldest books of the Bible by thousands of years was the Kabbalah.

Legend informs us that the Kabbalah is the emobdiment of the rare astrological wisdom which was salvaged from the Arlantean civilization and carried to Egypt by Hermes, most ancient philosopher, where he taught it to a select group.

The Kabbalah was divided into two parts, the Practical and the Theoretical. The latter was divided into the Dogmatic and the Literal.

The Literal was the science which taught a mystic mode of explaining sacred things by the use of the letters of words, and a reference to the numerical value of the letters of which the words were composed. The number of a name was simply the sum of the numerical values of the letters composing it.

This mystic mode was used by Apollonius when he wrote the Apocalypse (Revelation), and "He Phren (Lower Mind) was 666, while "Iesous" (Higher Mind) was 888.

According to the Kabbalah, Man is considered the Perfected Creation, and the symbols representing Prefected Creation are:
A --Earth, foundation of which all things are built
WA--Water, as in the Egg
KA--Air, breath of life
RA--Fire, animating element

The Sphinx

This takes us to the Four mysterious Beasts mentioned so often in the Bible. They are symbolized in the Sphinx, also in the Four Fixed Signs of the Zodiakos, and represent the above Four Elements of Creation, as follows:

1. Leo, Fire, Astral Radiation, Spark of Life
2. Eagle, Air, Breath of Life
3. Aquarius, Water, River of Life
4. Taurus, Earth, Body of Life.

These four zodiakal signs, with all their analogies, explained the one secret WORD hidden in all the sanctuaries of the ancient world. Moreover, the Secret Word was never pronounced;

it was always spelt, and expressed in four letters, JHVH, and pronounded Yod-He-Vau-He.

The biblical makers arbitrarily selected and added the vowels and made the word JEHOVAH (Exod.6:3). The word did not refer to a person or to a god, but to the Four Elements.

Tarot Card 4, The Emperor

Card 4 of the Egyptian Tarot is the The Emperor, who represented the Law of Four--the Four Elements.

"I am the Great Law, said the Emperor (God)
"I am the Secret Word, the Ineffable Name (God)
"The Four Letters of the Name are in me, and I am in everything.
"I am the Four Great Principles; I am in the Four Elements; I am in the Four Seasons; I am in the Four Quarters of the earth; I am in the Four Signs of the Zodiakos. I am action, resistance, completion, and result.
"For him who has found the way to see me, there are no mysteries on the earth.
"As the earth contains fire, water and air, as the fourth letter of the Ineffable Name contains the first three and itself becomes the first, so my scepter contains the complete triangle and bears in itself the seed of a new triangle."

The Four Elements

The Ancient Astrologers based their philosophy upon the Four Elements which permeate and compose everything. By discovering these Elements in all objects and phenomena of quite different catagories, between which the men of darkness sees nothing in common, the esoteric sees the analogy between all objects and all phenomena, and is convinced that all things are constituted according to the same law and the same plan.

The concept is definitely clear: If the Ineffable Name (Four Elements) is in everything, then everything must be analogous to the whole--the atom analogous to the universe, and all analogous to the Ineffable Name.

And here is where the church got its god. Just as the Sphinx symbolizes the Four Elements, so does the church god, but the world is not given that knowledge. The church says:
"By a paradox that defies the reasoning faculty, but which is readily resolved intuitively, God is apart from, and independent of, the universe, and yet he permeates every atom of it."

So true is the statement, and yet so misleading and deceptive. That is as far as theology goes. It does not attempt to analyze its God. To do so would destroy him. For God is just a word adopted by the church to conceal the facts from the masses.

Man's Constitution

The Ancient Astrologers taught that man's total constitution is compounded of modifications of the Four Elements, each of which contributes its part to him, and because of which he has conscious expression simultaneously in four different worlds, or in four phases of the same world.

Each of man's four bodies, electro-magnetical, vito-chemical, astrological, and Egoical, is charactered and symbolized by one of the Four Elements, the more sublimated ones interpenetrating the grosser, localizing the conscious functionism of all four in the lower one, man's physical body, to make him correspond to and harmonize with his physical environment.

The Astrologers said that man possessed a physical body which harmonizes with the earth, an emotional body which harmonizes with the water, a mental body with harmonizes with the air, and an astral body which harmonizes with the Fire.

Heraclitus said that man is Cosmic Fire imprisoned in a body of earth and water. Hermes said:

"He that looketh upon that which is carried upward as fire, that which is carried downward as earth, that which is moist as water, and that which bloweth as air,--how can he sensibly understand that which is neither hard nor moist, nor tangible nor perspicuous, seeing it is understood only in power and operation? But I pray to the mind, which alone can understand the generation and the constitution of man."

The same statement, in different phraseology, appears in the Bible: For the invisible things from the creation of the world are clearly seen (in the mind), being understood by the things that are made (visible) (Rom.1:20).

"Born of water" (Jn.3:5) embalms implications commonly disregarded and generally misunderstood. All birth in the natural world is in water. The human foetus develops in a sac of water. It emerges at birth from water into air.

All growing things must have water as a primary condition, or perish. That fact was used by the sagacious Astrologers as an index of birth of any kind.

Massey said: "Birth from the element of water was represented in the Ancient Mysteries by rebirth of the astral body from the water of baptism." That was the original meaning of baptism.

The biblical statements make no sense until this basic predication is made: That man exists not on one plane of nature, but on four, and that he makes contact with the actualities of each plane by means of a body that is composed of substance indigenous to each plane.

Man's focus of consciousness may pass from one to the other

of the four bodies under pressure of the swing of his interests.

When we speak of living within the whole range of our being, we are unwittingly repeating a conception of Astrology, the literal truth of which we have lost the data to comprehend. It was not lost, but deliberetely destroyed by the church.

Septenary Constitution

Revelation is a Book of Sevens because it deals with man's septenary constitution. The Book with Seven Seals symbolizes the human body (Rev.5:1). The book was copied from an ancient scroll written thousands of years before the world ever heard of the gospel Jesus. Every statement in that book referring to him is a suprious interpolation.

Of his septenary constitution, the man of darkness has degenerated to where he now deploys into function only the lower quaternary powers. He now develops only four of the ultimate seven bodies of his being for contacting the reality of all realms. And those are the four bodies typed by earth, water, air and fire.

It was declared astrologically that the atomic substance of which each of man's four bodies is composed is, in structural essence, a seven-fold attenuation or sublimation of the one which it interpenetrates.

Each one interpenetrates its coarser neighbor, and at the same time is interpenetrated by its next finer associate. So, the four weld together as one, occupying the same three-dimensional area, yet with a great gulf fixed between each, the abyss of difference of electronic vibration, wave length, frequency, and radial orbit.

This is the great gulf that divides each plane from the other. It is not a chasm of spatial distance, but a hiatus between vibrational frequencies, wave length and other forms of potency.

To bridge the abyss and step from one plane to another, it is requisite that man be able to tune up, or down, the mathematical "pitch" of his Consciousness, as exemplified by the "tuning in" process of the radio.

That was another secret taught the Neophyte in the Ancient Mysteries, and to which the entire book of Revelation is devoted. The biblical makers inserted many fraudulent interpolations to make the book refer to the church and its Jesus.

We are what our Consciousness is; and two discordant tones of Consciousness are not on the same plane, or in the same world. Their failure to harmonize puts them into different areas of the field of life.

Fire and Water

We can present this story more effectively by reducing the tetradical nature of man to the broad generality of the dualism of the two elements,--the Celestial and the Terrestrial in one body. These are the two bodies to which Paul referred when he said there is a natural body and also a spiritual (astral) body (1 Cor.15:44).

This arrangement makes the two most distinctive symbols Fire and Water. Their proper interpretation almost alone, reveals the Key to the ancient astrological texts.

We shall accept Fire to designate undeviatingly man's celestial segment, and Water his terrestrial portion. Or, Fire to connote the god of heaven, and water the earthly man.

In more condensed form, Fire may type the astral man and water the physical man.

Classifications so general are not to be considered scientifically precise, but they are correctly and systematically applicable, and without loss of explicit meaning.

Oddly enough, by one of these inversions to which the imagery is susceptible, the Serpent becomes a symbol of both the Fire and Water Elements, and hence represents both our astral and our sensual natures.

There was the Fiery Serpent of Moses, and the Water Dragon of Revelation; then the Good Serpent, Agathodaemon, and the Evil Serpent, Kakodaemon.

Water also becomes a dual sign, with a higher and lower translation: As the first, it was an emblem of the outpourings of divinity, the Water of Life that Jesus promised the woman at the well. As the second, it typed the fluctuating, restless, sensual nature in which the Divine Fire was so nearly extinguished.

Even Fire shares the dual meaning, for it symbols the Celestial Life, the Fire of Prometheus, Jove's thunderbolt, as well as the fires of the torture and hell of earthly existence.

The ancient Ritual mentioned man's baptism on earth, "in the Pool of the Double Fire." This is readily comprehensible, because of the shifting of the divine beings from the empyrean to the mundane sphere of activity.

In the astral world it was a pure, clear flame; in the physical world it is fed with damp, gross fuel, and becomes lurid in hue and charged with noxious gases, turning to steam and smoke.

The major part of the whole significance of man's incarnation can be seen reflected in the imagery of Fire introduced into a semi-water condition.

Man's earthly history is adumbrated by the picture of an imperishable spark of Astral Fire struggling to live and expand its power in a moist environment.

Our inmost essence is as a central nucleus of Fire striving valiantly to light a mass of wet wood--the physical body. The resultant smoke and smudge is the perfect type of our terrestrial life, intellectually and astrally.

These were the very symbols of man's terrene existence employed in Greek Philosophy, and destroyed by the church.

This peculiar duality of the symbols, discerned throughout, is itself a reflection of the duadical movement, or double status, of the Astral and the Physical.

For that which began as heavenly, passed into earthly embodiment, and the pertinence of the symbols had to change with the change of status. All the heavenly symbols became inwrought with earthly reference and imperfection, and thus gathered the implication of evil.

Man's lower nature was symbolized by the Astrologers as composed of the elements of earth and water, and his higher of air and fire. The body is about seven-eights fluid and the remainder solid.

Plotinus termed the descent of the Ego into the physical body "a fall into dark mire." The Psalmist said, "I sink in deep mire, where there is no standing. I am come unto deep waters where the floods overwhelm me" (69:2).

Fire plunged into water pointedly dramatizes the basic import of the whole incarnation procedure.

The Ego, a fiery nucleus of noetic intelligence, is plunged into the watery habitat of the fleshy body. The moral battle is a struggle between the Egoical Fire and the water of emotion and desire. The Fire wins the victory by heating up and drying out the heavy, humid nature of physical man.

The Fire of Life must dry out a path across the sea of generation, so the Ego may cross the reed (Red) sea out of Egypt (body), as also the Jordan River, into the Holy Land (Astral World) without wetting its feet.

The Egyptian Ritual said, "Oh; the Being dormant within his body, making his burning in flame, glowing within the sea of his vapor. Come, give the Fire, transport (transmute) the Vapor of thy Being."

Each higher element is able to raise the potential of the one below it, and refine it. So earth (sense) is raised and purified by water (emotion); water (emotion) by air (mind); and air (mind) by Fire (Ego).

This interpretation furnishes a key table of values. By this simple application in various combinations, a hundred intimate meanings of ancient symbolism may be resolved into comprehensible interpretation.

Water, not in its fluidistic form, is the first aspect of matter in all the oldest mythologies and cosmologies. It is the primal substance of the Universal Mother. Basically, mother, matter, and water are one. Plato mentions water as "the liquid of the whole vivification."

The interpenetration of the gross bodies by the subtler ones in man may be realistically depicted by the relations subsisting between the four elements of the external world.

Living physical bodies of earthly constituency hold water, and water embosoms air, and in the air is the hidden potency of fire. The four elements consistently interpenetrate each other, the finer in the coarser.

An eloquent symbol appears in view to edify the mind at the end of a shower--the rainbow. In its sevenfold coloration we read again the septenary design of all cosmic constitution, including the life of man.

The one essence of clear light, shining thru the descending waters (rain), is subdivided into seven constituent rays, revealing the Seven-Rayed God of the Ancient Astrologers.

All manifest forms are septenary in structure. Every cycle runs its course and comes to perfection in seven sub-cycles. The creation story in the Bible completes itself in seven days and seven nights. The Book with Seven Seals mentioned in the Bible represents man's body (Rev.5:1).

The Eternal reflects in the rainbow, at the end of the rain, in token of the saying, "never again will cosmic processes destroy mankind."

That is an allegory. For man, at the end of his sojourn in the watery habitat of his body, will have completed his perfection in seven stages, and will not need further immersion in the Sea of Generation. As the rainbow disappears with the end of the rain, so the sun reigns alone again in its one clear light.

A unitary ray of light, passed thru a three-faced glass prism and dividing into its seven colors, is a memorable certification of cosmic creational methods.

Man actually presents a three-faced transparent medium for the first light in the upper level of his nature to provide the requisite condition for this phenomenon in his life.

The immortal Ego itself has segmented already into a triad which hovers in the upper sphere of consciousness. It is the great Solar Triad of Consciousness-Mind-Intelligence, a reflection of man's constitution of the Cosmic Trinity. It is man's triangle of conscious faculty and is of bright essence. Thru it shines the one unbroken ray of Intelligence from the Primal Fount of Light, to be reflected on the physical screen of human life on earth, in a final sevenfold differentiation.

Astrological Wisdom expounds more intricate cosmic and evolutionary data than the greatest of modern scientists have yet discovered.

Nearer to man there is another application of the water symbol. The element is made to stand for the second of his constitutional principles, the emotional nature, which is so closely inwrought with his physical body as generally to include the latter in its reference.

This is the most suggestive and fruitful use of water as a symbol. It is the water of earth, of sense, of generation, that holds the threat of drowning the god. It is the water on which he must learn to walk without sinking, and symbolized by Jesus when he walked on the water (Mat.14:25).

Water is the aptest symbol of the lower nature because of its fluidic character and its constant motion and fluctuation, representing sense and emotion.

The Ego, cast amid the senses and the feelings, is in unceasing flux, as Heraclitus said. Like the restless waves of the sea, it is never still. No figure could better portray the dual sense-emotion-life of mortals than the heaving bosom of the ocean, or the moving current of a river.

Natural phenomena presents a marvelous textual illustration of the whole cyclical life process in the water-circulation system.

The ocean is the source of all rising water emanations. The sun raises hugh masses of moisture into the sky by its thermal power; and a reduction of temperature causes the vapor to condense and fall as rain. From remote highlands it flows into brooks, rivers, and bays, and finally returns to its home in the ocean.

This cosmic circuit of water bristles with analogies of the Cosmic Life Cycle at every turn.

The sun's function of lifting huge masses of invisible vapor into the sky, types the Ego's power to refine the invisible elements of Consciousness-Mind-Intelligence and elevate the substance of life.

The Invisible

The Bible states that the Invisible is greater than and superior to the Visible.

Paul said we look not at the things which are seen, but at the things which are not seen; for the things which are seen are temporal; but the things which are not seen are eternal (2 Cor.4:18).

Every phase of the Cosmic Cycle is visible except that one in which the water is lifted up again from the sea into the sky.

The entire circuit of the Cosmic Cycle is perceptible except that one arc in which matter is reduced to radiatory, vaporous form. In every round of the Cosmic Process, there is always that one invisible, unseen stage.

This fact holds a pointed moral for physical science. It is the unwillingness of physical scientists to recognize the reality of the Cosmic Cycle of Life in its invisible stage, that has locked physical science in darkness, plunged it into confusion, and produced the absurd theory of evolution.

This is the point where physical science contends that when the body ceases to function, that is the end of everything, that is annihilation.

Our conception of the Future Life is based upon the declaration that human life runs a similar cycle, in harmony with all cosmic processes, issuing from the invisible, subjective, radio-active realm into the visible, objective, palpable·life of the body, and retiring in order again to the invisible, astral realm.

Like the invisible vapor rising from the ocean, to fall again in gentle showers or torrential floods, the Living Ego rises from the body in death, is born again, and returns to its astral home in the Aeriferous Substance surrounding the earth, and its positive existence there is unseen.

And physical science stands firm on its denial of the Ego's subsistence after the death of the body on the sheer ground of its invisibility, its disappearance. It thus creates the darkness in which it flounders by refusing to grant and consider the reality of that which it cannot see, feel, smell, examine, weigh and measure.

Vitality-Consciousness-Mind-Intelligence

The quaternary qualities that make man are vitality, Consciousness, Mind and Intelligence. These qualities cannot be seen, felt, smelt, examined, weighed or measured. Yet they are realities. Physical science admits that.

Whence their source? The brain says physical science. But

the brain is material substance, and perishes along with the rest of the body at death.

Here is where we meet some strange astrological symbolism that appears in the Bible, the correct interpretation of which lies far beyond the ability of the priest and preacher.

The Bible says: Behold, a door opened in heaven (Rev.4:1). Or ever the Silver Cord be loosed, or the Golden Bowl be broken (Eccl.12:6). And Jacob dreamed, and behold a ladder set up on the earth and the top of it reached to heaven; and the angels were ascending and descending on it (Gen.28:12).

This symbolism reveals the wonderful secret of life to him who is able to interpret it correctly. We shall not go into this here, as we have covered the matter in detail in our work titled "Pre-Existence Of Man." Let it suffice to say that this biblical symbolism covers the very things we are discussing here,--the Cosmic Cycle of Life.

This symbolism teaches us that, like the invisible vapor that rises to the sky, so rises the Ego, ascending on Jacob's Ladder, to return to earth as the angels descending on Jacob's Ladder, and that the Ego is subsistent in the interim. For if it did not continue to exist, it could not return.

It was to hide this fact that the church fathers destroyed the ancient scriptures which dealt with that phase of life,-reincarnation.

As the water-cycle is complete in spite of the one invisible segment, so the cosmic cycle of Life is complete, with no arc missing.

The apparently missing link is found in the invisible realm. And even now physical science is discovering that the most vital, powerful and dynamic realities are those of the unseen world.

Water was the first visible creation, and up out of its depths came the emanating gods to get the breath of life.

There is no more astounding replica of this cosmic process than that furnished by the modus of human birth.

As the child is born, it issues into life out of a sac of water, and the first thing done by the attendant nurse is to stimulate the latent breathing function.

Stilling the Sea

The gospel Jesus calmed the wind and raging water (Mat.8:26).

Job said, "He stilleth the sea by his power," as did Horus, Tammuz, Jonah, and others. More allegory.

In quieting the storm, the gospel Jesus played the part of the Egyptian Horus in the Ritual, of whom it is written: "He hath destroyed the flood."

The parable of Herod in trying to kill the gospel Jesus by slaughtering the innocents is paralleled by Pharaoh, who attempted to eradicate the menace of the Israelites by ordering the mid-wives to kill all the male children at birth by drowning (Ex.1:22). This is an allegory depicting the danger menacing the Ego during incarnation in the watery region of the body.

Sargon said his mother gave him to the river, "which drowned me not." He drew me out of the waters, says the Psalmist. Moses (Mosheh) means drawn from the water (Exod.2:10).

In a myth of the island of Celebes, seven celestial nymphs descended from the sky to bathe. They were seen by Kasimbaha, who stole the robes of one of them named Utahagi. These robes gave Utahagi the power to fly, and without them she was caught. She became the wife of Kasimbaha and bore him a son.

Here the Ancient Astrologers preserved a legend of the highest value. For the robes stolen by man on earth represent the Immortal Astral Body.

The sign of Aquarius is the waterman pouring from an urn the water of life in a double stream. Ancient literature is filled with reference to the two waters, or the water of the double source. These indicate the two poles of positive and negative life.

Astral Fire

The origin of the word Fire goes back to the Greek pur (pyr). Massey traces the word "pyramid" from the stem, plus the Egyptian "met", meaning "ten" or "a measure", giving us "pyramet."

According to Massey, pyramet stands thus for the ten original measures or arcs traced by the fire god, the Sun, thru the zodiakal circuit.

As the great pyramid at Gizeh, and others, are related to sidereal measurements, this assertion of origin is plausible. The word would then mean "a ten-form measure of fire", a figure for manifest life.

The Greek pur goes back to the Chaldean "ur", primitive word for fire. To this, the Egyptians added their article "the" as a prefix, in the form of "p", making the word "pur".

So, Ab-Ram, as Prof. Hotema shows in "Ancient Sun God," came out of "Ur", the Primal Fire of Creation (25).

The Sanskrit Agni, god of fire, is traced by Massey to the general root "ag", meaning "to move quickly", as in the Latin "ago," to go, agile, active, agitate,etc.

As this derivation links fire closely with the Greek "theos" (god), who by etymology is the "swift runner," "the swift goer," Agni, god of fire, may well be connected with the "theos," the god whose symbol everywhere is the swift-darting shaft of fire.

That the Ego is a spark of the cosmic fire is attested by the words of the Speaker in the Ritual: "Lo, I come from the lake of flame, from the lake of fire, and from the field of flame, and I live."

The Chaldean Oracle said: "All things are the progeny of one Fire." The Bible says, "For our God is a Consuming Fire" (Heb. 12:29,etc.).

The heavenly fire, the Oracles affirm, did not shut up its power in matter, nor in works, but in Intellect. "For the artificer of the fiery world is an intellect of intellect."

A hail of stars or sparks over the earth was a typical figuration of the descent of the bright deities. The Egyptian ceremony of flinging a blazing cross into the Nile conveyed the same connotation.

A cross of fire thrust into water carried the purport of the sacrificial act of incarnation. A fiery serpent on the cross was a kindred emblem.

In the early church the cross of fire was adored on a Friday, when a lighted cross was suspended from the dome of St. Peter's, the cross being covered with lamps in a fire-traced figure.

The esoteric practice of burning animal flesh on a physical altar was the consuming by the divine flame of the cross that emanated from the carnal segment in man.

The fire god came into the natural body to transfigure it. To achieve this aeonial labor, the fire had to burn out slowly the grosser elements, earthy and moist, by astral alchemy and replace them by subtle and pure essence akin to its own diviner substance.

All man's lower emotionalism and heavier sensualism are as fuel for the burning. The lurid flare of such combustion is only turned to pure clear flame by pain and defeat.

Animal sacrifice upon an altar, frequently mentioned in the Bible, was only to dramatize the conversion of physical man to astral man under the action of fiery astral energies. And it is significant that the ancients swore not by the altar, but by the fire on the altar.

Man would not swear by the impermanent part of his nature, but by the stable and eternal. That was the Ego.

The inner fire, imprisoned in the body, strives to burn its way into flame. But the fuel is damp, like wet wood, and the flame must slowly dry out the resistant mass.

The element of fire was regarded as latent in both wood and stone, needing only force or heat to bring it forth into action.

Touch stone or steel to a spinning emery wheel and see the sparks fly. These substances are condensed astro-electricity. Heat will melt and vaporize all substances and return them to the astral state.

Fire, with its eternal intimation of the Ego, was regarded as the inner essence of all material substance, an ancient conception now endorsed by physical science.

We are told that the earth is a ball of fire, with a cooled crust on which we live. So, there can be no quibbling about the esoteric meaning of the narrative of Shadrach, Meshach, and Abednego, the three mentioned in the Daniel who were symbolically cast into the fiery furnace. It is another allegory of the solar triadic god, in the three principles of ego-mind-body, symbolized here as a fiery furnace.

The life of the ancient god, said Budge naively, "sometimes takes the form of a flame of fire." He continues:

"These ceremonies are said to be 'an exceedingly great mystery to Amenta, and a type of the hidden things of the other world.'"

Thus is the exoteric scholar's mind stultified by want of that one key to ancient symbolism: that this world is Amenta. For the mystery pertains to the hidden things of no other world than the world on which we live, with its two phases of material and immaterial.

The Flaming Sword

The flaming two-edged sword of the Garden of Eden, set to guard the Tree of Life (Gen.3:24), symbolizes man as a vase between the two fires of the material and immaterial worlds, the glowing fire of supernal splendor, and the lurid fire of infernal misery.

These are dual aspects of one fire. Hence, man's life is divided by that fire which catches him on both sides, upper and lower. The fire of life consumes in both directions. It lights and it burns. It glows in beauteous glory, or painfully consumed the lower self.

The flaming sword is the eternal emblem of the duality of man's nature.

A huge mass of testimony could be adduced from the Bible to stress the prominence of fire typology. Ezekiel saw fire, in the midst of which were the Four Beasts symbolized by the Sphinx (1:4-5). The Psalmist said: "Our God is a living fire." Paul wrote: "Our God is a Consuming Fire (Heb.12:29).

Stars are closely intermingled with fire symbolism. They are fiery in constitution, and typed one of the elementary creations, of which there seem to have been three, the first cosmic or universal, offering a sevenfold differentiation in primal substance; the second astral and planetary; and the third racial and individual in mankind.

Much of the endless confusion in the interpretation of the creation legends has risen from the failure to distinguish between which of these was being considered.

All ancient philosophy referable to man was based upon the human constitution of a septenate of powers. We see the first creation in the hebdomadal formation of all physical creation; the second in the septenary solar system; and the third in the human formed of the seven principles of natures.

Chapter 6

Astral World

The gullible multitude fails to realize that the Christian Bible was made for the church, not for the masses. The purpose back of the making of the Bible was to enthrone the church and to enslave the masses.

With that purpose in mind, the biblical makers employed every scheme imagainable in the compilation of their Bible to make it fit to serve their purpose. Hotema mentions this matter in his "Cosmic Creation" in these words:

"The Bible, compiled from ancient scrolls and manuscripts to support this scheme of profit and mass enslavement, is filled with hundreds of distortions and spurious interpolations, for the express purpose of making effective the scheme that was in the minds of the schemers who prepared the Bible for the church.

"We defy anyone to read one paragraph in the Bible and find in it either truth or falsehood separately stated.

"Each falsehood is inseparably connected with an undeniable truth, and the true and the false are so intricately and delicately interwoven, that it is absolutely impossible for the unprepared mind to separate the one from the other.

"The Bible has gone out to the world and chained in darkness and ignorance a larger mass of people than any other book has ever done, and those deceived people must live in that error and darkness until they evolve to such mental ability that they can winnow the true from the false in this book, and come to comprehend its falseness, as many have done."--p.47.

In order to conceal the fraud, the ancient scrolls were destroyed and huge libraries burned, and all countries controlled by the Roman Empire were plunged into intellectual darkness. That period of time was termed the Dark Ages, but more recently the term has been replaced by the milder term "Middle Ages."

The Ancient Masters developed a Science of Man, based upon their study of the heavenly bodies and cosmic phenomena, and it was called Astrology. It dealt with the astral world and the effect of astral radiation upon the earth and its inhabitants. It was observed and practiced in India for thousands of years before the compiling of the Vedas.

Blavatsky stated that the great astrologer of India was Asura-maya, who was born in Atlantis, thus testifying, upon the authority of the Puranas, to the extreme antiquity of Astrology.

Lucian asserts that Orpheus brought the principles of Astrology to Greece from India, and that the planets were signified by the seven strings of his lyre (Hall, p.19).

Paracelsus said: "The body of man is his home. The Architect who builds it is the Astral World; the workers are at one time Jupiter, at another Venus; at one time Taurus, at another Orion. Man is a Sun and a Moon and a Heaven filled with Stars. The World is a Man, and the Light of the Sun and the Stars are his Body. The Ethereal Body cannot be grasped, and yet it is Substance, because Substance means Existence, and without Substance nothing exists."

The Astrologers used the terms Astral and Celestial, the latter being a world derived from "ciel," a canopy.

We are told that as the church fathers made their Bible, they deleted the words astral, ethereal, and celestial, and interpolated spiritual, because the true meaning of the latter term was unknown to the masses.

The church fathers greatly feared Astrology as a means of exposing the source of their actor called Jesus, the Lamb of God, the head sign of the Zodiakos (Jn.1:29,36). So, they burned and destroyed the astrological scrolls, prohibited the study of Astrology, and condemned the Zodiakos as the work of superstitious heathens. As a result, Astrology became the most deplorable charlatanry.

According to Astrology, the Sun rules the sign of Leo, and Leo is the ancient sign of the Human Ego. Thus, the Solar Ego and the Human Ego are correlated.

The Zodiakos is an epitome of the creative process. It depicts in symbolism the process of the development from the central point to the periphery of the circumference.

The Traditional characters of the twelve types definitely and scientifically lend themselves to the creative drama of the zodiakal process. These astrological characters play a dialectical role, leading to the unfoldment in each of the four spheres of being, and bringing creative processes from potentiality to actuality.

When the church fathers condemned and outlawed Astrology, they had to dispense with the Astral World, the subject of Astrology. And this was the emergency and exigency which led to the adoption of the empty spiritualistic terminology.

According to the dictionary, spirit simply means "air set in motion by breathing." This logically means that when we call the church God "A Spirit" (Jn.4:24) we mean "air set in motion."

The occult works of the Astrologers are full of references to the Astral World, and yet the modern masses are kept in such darkness, that there are few who have any realization or comprehension as to what the Astral World is, and of what the Astral Body of man consists.

According to the Astrologers, the Astral World is the fourth dimensional plane which lies exactly relative to our material world, and was regarded as the Plane of Creation, or Formation, or Transformation. It is the Plane in which there pre-exists all the potential or invisible entities that appear in the visible world. It is a vast ocean of Aeriferous Substance containing the entities and elements from which the material world attracts all things that come into visible manifestation.

The Astral World of the Ancient Astrologers became the Heaven of Christianity, but no preacher can describe it.

What is the fourth dimension? Hotema discussed that at length in his "Kingdom of Heaven."

The material world in which we live is a realm of three dimensions,--that is three directions at right angles from a given point,--the dimensions of width, length, and height.

The occultist explains the fourth dimension by showing that the point, extended, becomes a line, and the line, extended, becomes a surface, and the surface, extended, becomes a solid. They say the fourth dimensional hypothetical figure would be the extension of a solid into another direction. What that direction is, they cannot say.

The Yogins hold that the fourth dimension is not one of extension outward, but rather of contraction inward, and that the Astral World may be found by the contraction of the Ego from the external world. If it contracts to a fine point, it finally passes into the borderland and disappears into the fourth dimension. That is what the Ego does at the death of the physical body.

The Soul's secret

The Astral Plane is the invisible world which contains the Virility of all Life and the Four Elements of creation.

The Astral, Fourth Dimensional Body, the Archeus, is the Ego, and its creative work is explained by Hotema in "Pre-Existence Of Man."

Just as the bony skeleton supports the flesh of the body, the Astral supports the entire body, and maintains and sustains the organs of the body, and supplies them with the vitality and qualities which are necessary for the sustenance of Life on the terrestrial plane.

The Astral Body begins its work of forming the physical body at the moment of conception, as Hotema has explained in Part II, Pre-Existence of Man" under the subhead, "Hidden Artist." There he has also explained what the Astral Body is.

The Astral Body is the Real Man, the Ego, and as he comes from the Astral World, there is no reason, except the false teachings of the church, why he should fear the creative process of death which releases him from the physical body so he may return to his original home.

All that man does is to change his consciousness from its focal point in the physical body to its focal point in the Astral Body. Paul mentioned the matter in these words:
"Behold, I show you a mystery: We shall not sleep (in death), but we shall be changed, in a moment, in the twinkling of an eye." (1 Cor.15:51,52).

Death of the body occurs when the Ego leaves it. Life is not the product of body function, BUT THE CAUSE OF IT. Life does not end when body function ceases, but body function ceases when Life leaves the body.

Fear of Death

The teachings of the church are designed to make men fear death. It is the fear of death that drives the masses into the church.

Men fear death because the church invented a terrible God as a judging, vengeful, terrifying God who shall punish, and punish, and punish us for each mistake we have made.

We do not understand death, and so become afraid of death. The church is careful to see that we do not understand death.

Death is not extermination. Death is not an ending, a finality. Death is the creative process of returning the Ego to a resting time - a joyful recognition of the Astral World, a place of peace and happiness.

But due to the false teaching of the church, we fear the

terrible punishment of a God of vengeance; we fear fire; we fear the final end where nothing remains; no evidence that we have been, nor shall be again.

So we cling to this little part, this short phase, this little time set aside from eternity, when we may have many, many times to live or "die"--as we would call it.

And it should not be a fearful thing, a thing of desperation, but rather a joyous greeting of things and places where we have been before but forgotten,--a beautiful resting time.

But we feel that death is the end. We talk and talk about eternal life, and then deny it vehemently with our doubts, our fears, our convictions that death is the end, a terrible end, as taught by the church.

Death is really a great release, a great freedom, a release from bondage--a recognition that death is not an ending, but a returning to a joyous time--a time of rest and understanding.

The chief objective of initiation in the Ancient Mysteries, that great school of Arcane Science, was to teach the "man of darkness" what he actually is, and explain to him that his return to his Primal Glory of Astral Existence comes thru the creative course of discarding his physical robe in the cosmic process called Death, which is fully as much of a creative process as that of being born in the flesh.

When the Ego leaves the physical body, it changes environment of necessity, or vehicle of light. The Ego sheds one envelope, in which it has prepared another.

The consciousness and vitality of the Ego are manifested by means of that vehicle in which it happens to reside. It is not consciousness and vitality that belong to the vehicle, but it is the vehicle that is used by them.

When the Ego descends from the Astral Plane, it clads itself to harmonize with its physical environment, but leaves that garment behind when it goes up.

When the body dies, the Ego is liberated from the law of gravitation, by which the body is bound to the earth.

Chapter 7

Enthusiasm for Death

The Future Life, which occupies so much space in ancient scriptures, seems to have suffered an eclipse in the races of the Mediterranean area, with the exception of the Egyptians, and then was reborn six or seven centuries before the Christian era.

The historians who have recorded the disappearance and return of the Future Life philosophy have confined themselves to a discussion of these strange phenomena without attempting to explain them and to seek out their determining causes.

The Ancient Mysteries, because they proclaimed the Existence of the Ego and guaranteed to it a future life, were greeted with so much enthusiasm, that the mystic cults sprang up in all the cities.

The happiness of the Future Life was the most inestimable prize. The Christians theory is erroneous that some phases of the Future Life are described in the 3rd and 4th verses of Chapter 21 of Revelation, to-wit:

"God shall wipe away all tears from their eyes; and there shall be no more death, neither sorrow, nor crying, neither shall there be any more pain; for the former things are passed away."

That is more allegory. Hotema shows in "Son Of Perfection" that this refers to the man who rises in the regeneration to the higher plane of Consciousness by the conquest of his animalstic nature, as stated in the 7th verse, to-wit:

He that overcometh (his animalistic nature) shall inherit all things (good in life); and I, Perfection, will be his Guide, and he shall follow me in health and happiness.

The gnostic poet Phocylides asserted that, "After we have left our earthly garments we shall be gods, for immortal and incorruptible souls dwell in us."

A tomb inscription at Petilia in Italy, which dates from the fourth century B. C., says, "Ah, it is a beautiful Mystery which comes to us from the blessed gods; for mortals, death is not an evil, but a good."

Enthusiasm for death was not only a funeral formula, but an infatuation which drove men to suicide.

"Life is but deceptions and miseries, vanity of vanities," declared Theognia.

Sophcles said, "The first of good things is to be born, and the second is to die as soon as possible.

The philosopher Cleombrotus of Ambracia threw himself from a

The Soul's secret

tower, that with a single leap he might enter the Future Life.

Hegesias of Cyrene, surnamed Peisithanatos (he who persuades to die), made a business of teaching that death was preferable to life. His disciples killed themselves in such numbers that Ptolemy Philadelphus closed his school and barred him from teaching at Alexandria.

Then the philosophers undertook to inquire into the nature of the Soul. Democritus formed it of subtile atoms, like those of fire, which are the most mobile of all. All the phenomena of life proceed from their movements, which agitate the whole body.

Heraclitus held that fire was the essence of all elements, circulating continually in all parts of the Universe, and he made fire the nature of the Soul.

Philosophers were so proud to possess a Soul that they took to despising the body. For Heraclitus it was an inert and inactive mass, which, when the Soul abandoned it, became an object of disgust. And so it is.

For Epicharmus, the Soul accomplished all functions of the body. It was the Soul that saw thru the windows of the eyes.

Euripides, who reproduces the ethereal idea of Orphism, sees in man only the Soul. He said, "The body is a possession which does not belong to us. Living, we inhabit it; dead, it must be returned to the earth."

Then the Soul, "reunited to the immortal ether, preserves a Consciousness that dies not."

Virgil gives information on the Soul's origin; the Souls of men and of animals proceed from the principle which penetrates, sustains, vivifies and moves heaven, the earth, the liquid plain, the brilliant globe of the moon, the sun and the stars.

Chapter 8

Allegory and Symbology

In occult or symbolic literature, there is one phenomenon of especial interest.

That is the Tarot, a very ancient work that escaped destruction at the hands of the Church because its symbolism was too complicated to be understood by those not familiar with the Secret Doctrine of the Ancient Astrologers.

The Soul's secret

Hotema explains in "The Mysterious Sphinx" that this document has come down to us as a deck of common playing cards, the four suits representing the Four Elements, and the two colors representing the Positive and Receptive forces of creation.

According to legend, the original pack of Tarot cards represented an Egyptian hieroglyphic book, called the Book of Thoth (Hermes), consisting of 78 tablets.

Even today parts of the figures of the Tarot can be seen in the ruins of the temples of Thebes, capitol of Egypt in 2000 B.C., especially on an ancient ceiling of one of the halls of the palace of Medinet-Abou.

The Church has seen to it that histories and encyclopedias do not tell the world that these Egyptian temples were destroyed by the Roman Army after the Roman State Church was established in the 4th century, the purpose being to obliterate the records and writings of the Ancient Astrologers.

In the great Alexandrian library, before it was burnt on orders of the Church, there were many copies of such books, consisting often, besides papyri and parchment, of a vast number of clay or wooden tablets.

We are told that in the beginning the Tarot cards were medallions stamped with designs and numbers, later metallic plates, then leather cards, and finally cards of paper.

Most of these were destroyed by the Church, which was and is ever alert to conceal from the eyes of the world the Astrological Wisdom, and to hide the fact that its religious system consists of an invention that was created by literalizing the ancient allegories and personalizing the ancient symbols.

Under the cunning hand of the Church, ancient fables became factualities and ancient symbols became personalities. The Ram of the Zodiakos became the Lamb of God (Jn.1:29,26), and heathenish Paganism became hellish Christianism.

Those who rejected the fraud were burnt and slaughtered, and, according to history, more than seventy million people were slain in the name of the gospel Jesus, the personalized Ram of the Zodiakos.

According to some commentators, the Tarot is a synopsis of the Hermetic Sciences with their various subdivisions, or an attempt at such synopsis.

All these ancient sciences harmonized and constituted a single system of psycho-bio-physiology study of Man and his relation to the world of noumena (astrological), and the world of phenomena (material).

The Bible

When the Church invented its fraudulent religious system in the fourth century, it needed a Bible to give it Holy Authority over the masses,--the authority of its mythical God.

This Bible was compiled in the Alexandrian library, where the workers has access to all the writings of the Ancient Astrologers.

Ptolemy Philadelphus (309-246 B.C.), a learned scholar of his time, offered rich rewards for all kinds of religious and philosophical scrolls and manuscripts.

Wise men of all nations, impelled by their desire for the reward, went to Alexandris with their best writings. In this way Ptolemy succeeded in securing some 280,000 of the most valuable scrolls and manuscripts in the world.

By comparing the various writings, Ptolemy was surprised to discover that all systems were approximately alike. They were copies of one original system, one universal religion and philosophy, which varied in different countries only as the customs of the people varied.

Traces of this very ancient system are preserved in inscriptions on stone monuments and temples of all races and all nations, in spite of the destructive work of religious fanatics, who strive to make their system appear as the only true one.

So, the Holy Bible of the Church was made in the Alexandrian library, by skilfully distorting the ancient scriptures as the workers copied them, to make them build up and refer to the Church God in the sky, to his Son Jesus on the earth, and to a cringing puppet called Man.

This is the way that allegory became literalism, symbology became personalism, Paganism became Christianism, and the King of the earth who, according to that Bible itself, has dominion over every living thing on the earth because of his superior intelligence (Gen.1:28), became a lowly worm that needed a savior to salvage his lost Soul from eternal torment.

He that believeth what the Church teaches and is baptized shall be saved; but he that believeth not shall be damned, says the Church in its Bible (Mark 16:16).

It was the most diabolical, infernal, atrocious crime ever perpetrated upon mankind in all the history of the world.

Wheel Of Life

Card No. 10 of the Tarot represents a wheel, called the Wheel of Fortune and also the Wheel of Life. The word Tarot means a wheel or something that rotates.

The Soul's secret

This wheel represents the Zodiakos, an ingenious symbol that is the product of ages of research, study and discoveries by the Ancient Astrologers of Man's relation to the Universe. It is a chart that represents the perpetual motion of the fluidic Universe and the flux of human Life.

This wheel in ancient symbology is pivoted upon the upper end of a staff, while at the base are two entwined serpents, representing Life manifesting its dual qualities, positive and receptive.

Poised with outstretched wings above the top of the Wheel is the Sphinx, the symbol of the quaternary constitution of man as we have explained.

The figure has the paws of a lion, and in its right paw it holds a sword, a symbol of power or authority. It is crowned with the symbol of Venus.

On the right side of the Wheel appears Anubis, symbol of Good, ascending, bearing in his right hand the Magic Wand of Mercury (Caduceus), and having on his head the symbol of Mercury.

On the left side of the Wheel appears Typhon, Egyptian god of Evil, descending with a trident in his hand.

These two figures on the Wheel indicate that Good is ever aspiring and ascending, while Evil is ever descending into darkness and disintegrating.

Anubis and Typhon represent Good and Evil, and indicate that Evil must descend and be disintegrated so that its force may rise and manifest as Good at the next upward turn of the wheel.

The Astrologers taught what physical science has recently discovered, that all things in the universe travel in circles, making the end and the beginning one and the same. As, the sun sets as it rises, and rises as it sets.

The Astrologers applied this cosmic law to Life and Man, and declared that man dies in the astral world as he is born in the physical world, and dies in the physical world as he is born in the astral world.

That is the Soul's Secret, and that is the substance of the Inner Doctrine that was symbolized in the Wheel of Life.

So, according to the Wheel of Life, man is bound and ruled by a ceaseless circle of births and deaths,--the Law of Reincarnation taught in all the ancient religions and philosophies, and condemned by the Church because it eliminates the service of its Jesus as the Savior of Souls.

"For God so loved the world, that he gave his only begotten Son, that whosoever believeth in him should not perish, but have

The Soul's secret

everlasting life" (Jn.3:16)

The Law of Reincarnation applies to Man as an Ego, that is the Astral Body, which is related to but separate from the physical body.

Nowhere in the Universe is there any such thing as the extinction and dissolution of anything, except the various formations.

Man's body is composed of substance as eternal as the sun, and moves in circles, just as the Ego does.

Every basic atom, science shows, is in a process of change into some other form of substance, and has its cycle of existence.

The Ego travels in a cycle, from birth into the physical world when a baby is born, to birth into the astral world in the creative process called death.

For death is equally as much of a creative process is birth is, and was so taught by the Astrologers.

The Astrologers ripped the veil of illusion from the face of things as they seem to be, so they could study them in their true nature and aspect in the relation to Cosmic Unity.

Their basic teaching was, that this earth, while it has form, shape and substance, and is activated by cosmic force, is really an appearance only, an illusion. In other words, what we see is the illusion and not the Reality of the world in which we live.

When we look at man we are deceived by his appearance. We cannot see a form of four parts. Yet man is composed of four bodies, not one. These bodies Hotema has listed in "The Flame Divine" as astral, aerial, fluidal, and physical.

Of the four bodies, the Astral or Ego is the Real Man. He inhabits a temple composed of aerial, fluidal and physical substance, which, combined, appear as the physical body. Behold the illusion.

These facts were taught the Neophyte in the Ancient Mysteries, and this knowledge dissipated the obscuring fogs which prevent the Man of Darkness from understanding what he really is and what he is not.

It was necessary for the Church to destroy this Ancient Wisdom in order to keep man in darkness and make him believe that he is a lowly worm that needs a Savior to salvage his lost Soul from eternal torment.

In the orthodox Christian theology man is taught that the Soul (Ego) is not immortal in its own right, but may acquire immortality if a man will entertain a certain belief,--the most preposterous proposition and the biggest falsehood that was ever invented.

And according to this lying dogma, the Soul that becomes immortal as the result of a certain belief, had no previous existence. It was born in the body, and the Immortal rises from the Mortal provided a man will entertain a certain belief.

Men of science who are materialists and evolutionists, hold there is no such thing as a Soul (Ego),--that man's life, consciousness, mind and intelligence are the result of chemical and mechanical energy.

According to these scientists, man's intelligence rises as pure chance of the physical structure and chemical balance of the body.

Physical science holds that when man, that is the physical body, dissolves and returns to its component elements, that the personality of the individual ceases to exist. That is the end.

That theory is contradictory to every basic law of the universe. For the universal and unvarying law of Force and Matter is, that no Matter and no Force are ever destroyed or lost. Nothing ends. These only change form and manifestation.

How would physical science answer this question. Why are life, consciousness, mind and intelligence, the qualities that make man, the exception to every known law of the Universe?

The very fundamentals of logic and reason must prove the persistence of the individual Ego, Entity, or Consciousness, after the physical body passes thru transition or death. Nothing begins and nothing ends.

Science has demonstrated that all things, past and present, are the product of cosmic processes that operate according to fixed and unchangeable laws.

The work of science is to trace by logical processes the relations between causes and effects, showing what causes produce what effects, in order that we may explain the effects and determine their causes.

Science to be valuable must be practical. Its province is to confer power. Knowledge is power. It must be something more than speculations regarding cosmic phenomena.

Phenomena could not exist except thru the forces of production. But these forces could accomplish nothing definite unless directed to their accomplishment. The process is Motion, the product is Matter, and both of these exist in accordance with law.

If it were possible to conceive that Force were undirected,

or irregularly directed, --if water were attracted now downward, then upward, and anon were destitute of direction; if steam represented contraction as well as expansion; and so of all forces if they were irregular in their operations, no definite work could be done.

If the universe, or any part of it, were the product of chance, or of an infinite succession of chances, the orderly arrangement of its parts becomes the most stupenduous miracle ever presented for human contemplation.

And furthermore, as the whole is made up of the parts, so we are warranted in asserting that the whole was produced as the parts are produced, and vice versa.

It is inconceivable that there is one order of work for the whole, with a contrary order for the parts.

We assert the doctrine that all are parts of one stupendous whole. All phenomena are the product of force, and all phenomena contain force. And so, it is the force IN the thing that produced it, and not the force from without.

Two and two make four only because they are included in the four. Oxygen, hydrogen and chemical affinity make water only because they are included in the water. Hence, it is a universal fact of observation, that all causes are interior as well as anterior to their effects.

The force of every explosion resides in the thing which explodes, and not in the accident which occasioned the explosion.

From an interior, invisible principle outward to results, is the process of existence without an exception in the universe.

Exceptions are in the realm of speculation and theology. It is impossible to conceive that the Unchangeable Processes, in the production of phenomena, have ever dropped a thread or failed to include universal existence in one grand plan.

Mathematicians do not record exceptions; mechanical laws know no exceptions. In a word, Cosmic Laws are invariable, universal, and omnipresent.

While the fact that all things in the universe are from one universal source, the process of their production illustrates a hazy indefiniteness in both the theologic and scientific mind that is remarkable.

In harmony with the law that governs all universal entities and elements, the Astrologers taught that the Ego is eternal. Nor is it formed in the body as taught by theology. In some form or nature it has existed always and will continue to exist indefinitely.

The Soul's secret

The Ego did not have an absolute beginning. For if it had a beginning, it would have an ending and could not be eternal.

In the Tibetan Secret Doctrine, and in the esoteric work of the Hindus, Yogas, Brahmins and other ancient races, there appears the reason for the doctrine of Reincarnation.

They held that there is an absolute conservation of all things. Nothing is wasted nor destroyed. Everything exists forever, even though its form may be changed.

They contended that the Ego is eternal; that it appears in the physical body at the time of conception in the mother's womb, --not for the first time in any birth, but as one of the many births which it has experienced in the past, and will in the future.

The biblical makers tried to exclude from their Bible all references to Reincarnation. They had to do it to provide a job for their Jesus. He was the Savior of Souls; but if Reincarnation were the regular course of creation, no Savior of Souls was needed.

Then, in spite of their caution, they made a slip when they let their Jesus talk about Reincarnation. They made him say, This man, John the Baptist, is Elias (Elijah) who was for to come (Mat.11:11-14,etc.).

This John the Baptist was the reincarnation of Elias (Elijah) of the Old Testament. That passage gives the whole thing away. It shows they had not been taught that the Soul is created new for each physical body, as Christianity asserts. The Soul is eternal and needs no saving.

Biblical Makers Tricks

A typical example of the tricks employed by the biblical makers to confuses the masses, in which ancient symbols are puzzlingly presented in the Bible, appears in the wild and sensational stories of the Zodiakos and the Sphinx in the Ezekiel and the Daniel, where the scribes have visions and dreams and see strange things which they record.

Only an occultist who understands the correct interpretation of ancient symbolism can read the first chapter of the Ezekiel and the seventh chapter of the Daniel and understand that the startling sights and objects there mentioned, are nothing more than the Zodiakos and the Four Elements which constitution man, and symbolized by the Sphinx and mentioned many times in the Bible.

The Four Beasts mentioned in the Bible always represent the Sphinx, and the Sphinx represents the Four Elements of which man is constituted: Fire, Air, Water, and Earth.

In the 4th chapter of Revelation the Zodiakos is mentioned

as "a rainbow round about the throne," with 24 seats and 24 elders sitting, which represent the 24 hours of the day, with 7 lamps of fire burning before the throne, which represent the 7 major nerve ganglia of man's body, and the Four Beasts round about the throne represent the constitution of Man (Rev.4:3-7).

The Seven Major Nerve Ganglia of the body are truly the Lamps of Life, as Hotema explained in The Flame Divine.

The reader will always do well in keeping his balance by constantly remembering that Man is the subject of the ancient scriptures, and not the God and Jesus of the Church.

The God and Jesus angles were cunningly woven into the Bible by the biblical makers as they prepared the Bible for the Church, and then all the ancient scriptures were destroyed to hide from the eyes of the world the biggest fraud in all history.

Ezekiel the priest looked, and, behold, a whirlwind came out of the north, a great cloud, and a fire infolding itself. Also out of the midst thereof came the likeness of four living creatures.

Now, as I beheld the living creatures, behold one wheel upon the earth by the living creatures, with his four faces, and the appearance of their work was as it were a wheel in the middle of a wheel (Ezek.1:4-16).

Much hogwash and hokum about nothing.

Old Daniel saw four beasts come up from the sea, diverse one from another. These great beasts, symbols of the Four Elements which constitute Man, are four kings, which shall rise out of the earth (Dan.7:3-17).

More hogwash and kokum. But old Dan failed to see the wheels which old Zek saw.

Man, rising his head suddenly, saw in the midst of the sky an immense revolving circle covered with kabballistic letters and signs.

The circle (Zodiakos) revolved with great speed, and together with it, now rising and now falling, revolved the figures of the serpent and the ram, and on top of the circle sat the Sphinx.

At the four quarters of the sky he saw on the clouds the Four Beasts of the Apocalypse,--one like a lion, another like a bull, the third with the face of a man, and the fourth like a flying eagle,--and each was reading an open book.

This is the Book with Seven Seals (lamps of fire burning before the throne), mentioned in the 5th chapter of Revelation, described in detail by Hotema in "Son Of Perfection."

And he heard the voice of the animals of Zarathustra:

The Soul's secret

"Everything goes, everything returns; eternally rolls the wheel of being.

"Everything dies, everything is born again; eternally runs the year of being.

"Being begins in every Now, around every Here rolls the sphere of There. The middle is everywhere. Crooked is the path of eternity."

Tarot Card #13 is titled Death. The mystery of Death is held in the Wheel of Life, and revealed by the journey of the Sun which, setting on the one side, rises on the other, being born again as it dies (Jn.3:3,5,7).

Life, Death, Sunrise and Sunset--these are but the illusions and fears of the man of darkness.

The Tarot is said to be the Key that unlocks the secret doctrines of the philosophies of the Ancient Astrologers, and was called the Arcana or the Clavicles of Solomon (Solar Man).

It is symbolized by a Key whose head is a circle containing the Four Fixed Signs of the Zodiakos, and symbolized in the Sphinx as the Lion, the Bull, the Eagle, and the head of Divine Man, The Flame Divine, also called the Angel.

You Must Believe

Christianity rests entirely and exclusively upon this statement:

"For God so loved the world that he gave his only begotten Son, that whosoever believeth in him should not perish, but have everlasting life" (Jn.3:16).

That statement carries no weight with a person who can think, for he notices at once that no law nor creative process is involved or cited to coroborate this bald statement. Accordingly, Christianity is not based upon any law and order, but entirely upon belief.

All law, order and creative processes are ignored and disregarded. They must be. They are never mentioned. They are of no value, but are dangerous to Christianity, whose fraudulent nature is exposed as soon as law, order and creative processes receive attention.

And the deceived millions are the willing slaves of Christianity because they hope that a belief will change cosmic law and give them "everlasting life."

And to hold the misled masses in that state of mind, they are kept in darkness as to the nature of Life, of Man, and of the Soul.

The Soul's secret

To conceal the Soul's Secret from the masses, billions of dollars have been expended, millions of people have been tortured and slain, and the most valuable records of the ancient world have been ruthlessly destroyed.

The motives back of this work of terror and blood were greed, profit, and power. It was done to enthrone the church and to enslave the masses. It was done to make it possible for the Church to sell to the masses its God in the sky and its Jesus on the earth.

The educational systems of the Christian world have been planned and prepared by the Church. The job has been so well done that even the great scientists of the present century know as little about the nature of Life, of Man, and of the Soul as the common layman.

One of these renowned scientists was Dr. Alexis Carrel. He said: "Each one of us is made up of a procession of phantoms, in the midst of which there strides an Unknowable Reality" (Man The Unknown 1935, p.4).

Another was Dr. Robert A. Millikan, head of the California Institute of Technology. He wrote:
"I cannot explain why I am alive rather than dead. Physiologists can tell me much about the mechanical and chemical processes of my body, but they can not say why I am alive" (Collier's, Oct. 24, 1925).

This astounding ignorance rises from the fact that it was planned that way by the Church. The Ancient Wisdom was destroyed to produce this ignorance; and modern scientists are reared and educated in an atmosphere designed by the Church to keep the mind in darkness and to perpetuate this ignorance.

The few aberrants who break thru the wall of darkness and find the Light of Knowledge are silenced, persecuted, jailed, eliminated, disgraced, and assassinated.

Most of Sir Isaac Newton's biographers have suppressed the fact that throughout his life, theology was much more important to him than science, and moreover, theology of a peculiar acrid and bigoted order. He felt constrained to make his most abstruse mathematical discoveries agree as far as possible with the dogmas of Christianity. And the whole general tendency then was, to test knowledge by the authority of the Church, and not the authority of the Church by knowledge.

Dr. Ernest Jones, British psychiatrist, mentioned these things in the Saturday Review, August 10, 1957. He wrote:
"There was an astonishing contrast between the extreme credulity Newton displayed concerning the literal statements of the Old Testament and the skepticism he evinced concerning the cardinal doctrine of the New. He followed Bishop Ussher in dating the creation from 4004 B.C., and on that basis and the data about the longevity of the patriarchs, he spent years in conjecturing

up a chronological history of all nations of the world in the course of which he reached unbelievable fantastic conclusions. He was especially engrossed in unraveling the obscure symbolism of the books of Daniel and Revelation. From the former he deduced that the tenth horn of the fourth beast must refer to the Roman Catholic Church, and confidently predicted its downfall in the year 2000."

Facts and Fancies

Those who fear to face the facts of Life should not follow us. If you depend upon faith and belief to save you from the consequences of your evil acts and deeds, this is not written for you.

In our quest of the facts of Life, consistency of thought demands that we proceed in our course in a direct manner thru infinite time to infinite results. We shall follow the facts to their utmost bounds, even tho it means the sacrifice of all the consecrated dogma of theology and ethics.

The progress of knowledge, even at this time, is impeded by the principle that there are kinds of knowledge which are dangerous, and the first question to be asked of the teacher of what appears as a new doctrine, is not "Can you prove it by means of facts," but rather, "What will its effect be upon the accepted systems of theology and ethics?"

The syncophancy of our academic pedants makes it possible for its brothers to live and thrive. And why this syncophancy of the academic? This at once leads us directly to Rome. Yes, all roads lead to Rome, as they have for centuries; and the tentacles of Rome extend into every Christian country on earth.

For instance, if a professor would overtly teach what he knew, the president of the institution would immediately have to dismiss him,--either this, or be dismissed himself by the powers above him; and the powers above him--the trustees, the city administration, the board of education, etc., are all responsible to the Vatican, either because the people are themselves Roman Catholic and ruled by the powers of the Vatican, or, what is more likely, they are beholden to Rome for votes and political appointments.

The cycle continues ad nauseum. Other pertinent examples that could be presneted as a perface to individual inspection, are newspaper blackmail, general censorship of text books, magazines, movies, etc., religious tests for public office, etc. etc. etc.

Chapter 9

The Man of Darkness

"The third century marked the end of classical rationalism, and the fourth marked the beginning of medieval (church) superstition,"--wrote F. A. Ridley, in "Evolution of the Papacy."

So, that was the end in Europe, Asia Minor, Egypt, and the entire Roman Empire of the Arcane Science of the Ancient Masters, handed down from the mists of antiquity.

From there on, learning and knowledge vanished in that vast region, and people sank into indescribable squalor and ignorance, with the advent of the Dark Ages, and the Sun of Science was not to rise again for more than a thousand years.

Then, in the 16th century the work of Martin Luther began the movement that led to the origin and growth of Protestantism, and the curbing of the despotic power of the Mother Church.

During those long centuries of darkness and nightmare, of horror and persecution, of faggot and blood, humanity stumbled blindly on, and the Mother Church, with Bible in one hand and bloody sword in the other, taught man to believe that he is lower than the most despicable worm.

By trickery, fraud and falsehood, forced upon the ignorant masses as the "Word of God," the Church enveloped man in a psychic atmosphere that constrained him to believe that he is hopelessly lost in the thraldom of sin, and headed for the most horrific perdition and punishment possible to imagine, unless he meekly and slavishly acknowledges all this to be true, and cringingly clings to the gown of a mythical Savior, presented by the Church as the only begotten Son of an anthropomorphic God (Jn.3:16), which was invented to serve as a terrifying monster to scare the wits, common sense and reason out of humanity.

Man has been born and reared in this atmospheric ocean of fraud and falsehood so long, and subjected to this degrading and hideous superstition for so many ages, that he is saturated with it thru and thru, to the point where no other line of thought, or the Light of Tuuth, can reach him--exactly as the Church has it planned.

This "sinner of darkness," whose powers of analytical reasoning have been befogged ever since his infancy, is so hopelessly engulfed in the treachery and trickery of the Church, that he is afraid to consider and weigh any other philosophy, feeling sure in advance that it cannot be true, and that to hearken to and heed it would only add to his future punishment, torment and torture.

This deceived man preys for peace in a world of strife, resulting from the struggle for power of the various religions, factions, systems, and organizations, and believes that the gospel Jesus will some day float in on the clouds, solve everything, and reign for 1000 happy years (Rev.20:4).

There is little hope or help for the deceived, unthinking masses so long as the Church can hold them in such abject slavery, and make them believe the lies and falsehoods it teaches, and which are repudiated by the Bible itself.

Lord of the Earth

What can be done to make man lift up his head and realize that, according to the Ancient Scriptures, he is the greatest being on the whole earth, and the greatest entity of all creation?

According to the Bible, man is so great in his own right that he has complete dominion over all the earth, and over everything on the earth, and under the earth, including the fish of the sea, the fowls of the air, the beasts of the field, and every living thing that moves upon the earth (Gen.1:26).

No God ever gave that right and power of dominion to man. It is his own rightful, inherent possession, his birthright, and it cannot be taken away from him by any power in the universe.

What has that man to fear? Why should he fear the hereafter? His future state is fixed and ruled by the same law that prepared the way for his coming into the world, and has also prepared the ways and means for his going out of it? That law is definite and certain and cannot be modified nor changed by any power in the universe.

Man, greatest of all creators, actually possesses within himself all the powers, systems, planets, and globes of the universe. The cells of his body are composed of atoms, and the atom is a tiny universe itself.

Man, the Microcosm, is the child and the image of the Macrocosm. The Ancient Masters said, "That which is above is like that which is below," and vice versa.

That ancient statement was changed by the Bible makers to cause the man of darkness to believe that he was created by the church God, in the image of the God:--
"So God created man in his own image" (Gen.1:27):

That misleading statement was never written by the Ancient Masters.

Science shows that man is the image of the Macrocosm, for he embodies the Seven Planes of Being: (1) electronic, (2) atomic, (3) molecular, (4) cellular, (5) organic, (6) animalistic, and (7) angelistic.

www.ingramcontent.com/pod-product-compliance
Lightning Source LLC
LaVergne TN
LVHW050938080826
845145LV00004B/1322
9781585093977